The Truth is Longer than a Lie

of related interest

Childhood Experiences of Domestic Violence
Caroline McGee
Foreword by Hilary Saunders
ISBN 1 85302 827 4

Reaching the Vulnerable Child
Therapy with Traumatized Children
Janie Rymaszewska and Terry Philpot
Foreword by Mary Walsh, co-founder and Chief Executive of SACCS
ISBN 1 84310 329 X

A Practitioners' Tool for Child Protection and the Assessment of Parents
Jeff Fowler
ISBN 1 84310 050 9

Managing Men who Sexually Abuse
David Briggs and Roger Kennington
ISBN 1 85302 807 X

Domestic Violence and Child Protection
Directions for Good Practice
Edited by Catherine Humphreys and Nicky Stanley
ISBN 1 84310 276 5

Therapeutic Approaches in Work with Traumatized Children and Young People
Theory and Practice
Patrick Tomlinson
Foreword by Paul van Heeswyk
ISBN 1 84310 187 4
Community, Culture and Change 14

Culture and Child Protection
Reflexive Responses
Marie Connolly, Yvonne Crichton-Hill and Tony Ward
ISBN 1 84310 270 6

The Truth is Longer than a Lie
Children's Experiences of Abuse and Professional Interventions

Neerosh Mudaly and Chris Goddard

Jessica Kingsley Publishers
London and Philadelphia

MT

First published in 2006
by Jessica Kingsley Publishers
116 Pentonville Road
London N1 9JB, UK
and
400 Market Street, Suite 400
Philadelphia, PA 19106, USA

www.jkp.com

Library of Congress Cataloging in Publication Data
Mudaly, Neerosh, 1950-
    The truth is longer than a lie : children's experiences of abuse and professional interventions / Neerosh
Mudaly and Chris Goddard.
        p. cm.
    Includes bibliographical references and index.
    ISBN-13: 978-1-84310-317-2 (pbk. : alk. paper)
    ISBN-10: 1-84310-317-6 (pbk. : alk. paper) 1. Child abuse--Treatment. I. Goddard, Chris (Christo-
pher) II. Title.
    RC569.5.C55M83 2006
    362.76--dc22

                            2005036454

British Library Cataloguing in Publication Data
A CIP catalogue record for this book is available from the British Library

ISBN-13: 978 1 84310 317 2
ISBN-10: 184310 317 6

Printed and bound in Great Britain by
Athenaeum Press, Gateshead, Tyne and Wear

7/12/07

The title for this book came from a 12-year-old girl who participated in a child abuse study and who had experienced sexual abuse and serious family violence. The full quotation from her reads as follows:

> that's always the problem with these people, they don't want to believe the truth, they just want to believe the easiest side, the side that is…the simplest, basically… They don't want to hear the truth because the truth is so much harder to understand and so much longer than a lie about the truth.

This book is dedicated to this child and the other children who participated in the study. They shared their views on their experiences of abuse and professional interventions.

Contents

Acknowledgements

This book is about child abuse and is presented mostly in the voices of children who have been abused. Inspiration for this book was drawn from the courage of the many children we worked with who had been abused and who demonstrated such strength in utilizing therapy for their healing and recovery. We want to acknowledge in particular the courage and enthusiasm of the children who participated in our study on which this book is based. The research demonstrated to us that, given the opportunity, children who have been abused have the ability to clearly communicate their views about even very traumatic experiences that affect them. As one 11-year-old child said after the research interview:

> I think people would be surprised if kids had the chance to talk...I mean...that's good that you're not getting the adults interviewed to see what they think, instead to get the kids interviewed from a kid's point of view. No one knows kids better than the kids.

We have been truly inspired by the struggles of these and other children to make sense of the abuse they have suffered and to reconstruct their lives.

Funding support was received in part from the Monash University Research Fund and we express our sincere thanks for the support of the University throughout this research.

We would also like to recognize Jessica Kingsley Publishers for their commitment to promoting pioneering types of literature. We are grateful for their interest in our work and their support during the publication process.

We convey our heartfelt appreciation to the Australian Childhood Foundation, first for the work it undertakes with children, young people and their families who have had a range of abusive experiences, and second for permitting us to undertake this research. Our special thanks to Dr Joe Tucci, the Executive Director, for his interest, support and belief in our research and in promoting the voices of children. Through his leadership, the Foundation continues to remain committed to providing truly child-centred services to children and young people in a way that is empowering to them and respects their feedback.

Thank you to our many colleagues, Bernadette Saunders, Janet Stanley, Janise Mitchell, Angela Weller and Lilian De Bortoli. Also Maree Waterworth and our many other fellow counsellors who constantly reassured us about the value of our work. We express our sincere appreciation to Dr Lydia Senycia for proofreading this book and for her valuable comments. Finally we wish to thank our families and friends for accommodating our moods and frustrations, and our unavailability over the years – in particular, Bala and Vishnu, and Lydia, Tom, Michael, Sandy and Julia.

CHAPTER 1

The Power of Children's Voices

I think people would be surprised if kids had the chance to talk...I mean...that's good that you're not getting the adults interviewed to see what they think, instead to get the kids interviewed from a kid's point of view. No one knows kids better than kids.

11-year-old female

Introduction

Towards the end of a therapy session, Sandy (not her real name) raised her head from her play with the dolls and said 'I love my mummy but I don't like Jenny. I live with Aunty Kath now and when I a big girl, I go live with my mummy.' This child had not only made sense of her mother's mental illness (she had begun to refer to her mother by name, Jenny, when her mother was ill, and as 'mummy' when she was well), but she had also worked out where she would be best cared for. Sandy was just four years old at the time.

Many children struggling with and attempting to make sense of their experiences of abuse are encountered in therapy. The voice of Sandy has come to mind more than once while listening to other children. With this recollection has come the realization that as child advocates and therapists we may have campaigned in all earnestness on behalf of children who have been abused but, nonetheless, we may have done these children some disservice in our zeal. We may have relegated the right of these children to be directly heard by usurping their authentic voices and, in doing so, denied them the opportunity to recount their experiences. This book is part of an emerging approach in research that aims to give children a voice on their experiences of abuse and violence (see, for example, Butler *et al.*, 2003; McGee, 2000). Children 'want to talk' and, when given the opportunity, may tell us what help they need (McGee, 2000, p.7).

We have been professionally involved for nearly three decades with children who have experienced abuse and family violence. With the passing years, we have been struck by the number of children who have demonstrated an ability to make sense of their experiences of abuse and about which interventions had been helpful to them. This sobering realization was largely the spur to our professional interest in wanting to research and document the children's experiences of their abuse as remembered by them, the impact of that abuse on them, and how they experienced support and response from significant adults, therapists and the protective system established to intervene and help them. Our main intention, however, was to empower children who had been abused by giving them an opportunity to have their voices heard.

Our research interests in child abuse and child protection also arose directly from our practice, just as we have advocated politically and publicly for the voices of children who have been abused to be heard.

The need for this book, and its aims

This book reports on a research study that sought the views of children and young people who had been abused on various aspects of their experiences of abuse.

Although children, when taken as a group, are at a higher risk of victimization than adults, research into the victimization of children has been inconsistent and less explored (Finkelhor, 1994,1997). The recent trend of obtaining feedback from consumers of welfare services is increasingly being viewed as critical to providing relevant and cost-effective services (Wise, 1995). Yet research involving children who have been abused has continued to be neglected. Amid professionals crossing swords, it is hardly surprising that the voice and the experience of the child who has been abused are the most silenced of all. The reasons for this may be that professionals have experienced difficulty in talking with the child (Doyle, 1997a; Goddard, 1996) or that children's legal and social dependence, and concerns about their competence 'mean that, in most spheres, modern childhood in Western European countries is characterised by protection and exclusion' (Finkelhor, 1994, p.4). Butler *et al.* (2003, p.13) argue that adult attitudes to children, which they refer to as the 'middle years conspiracy', may be caused by the fact that we 'simply do not want to hear' what children say, because the older generation want to retain their privileged position in society.

The legal view that children are incapable of critical decisions on matters that affect them has begun to be challenged by researchers, jurists, policymakers and scholars (Weithorn and Scherer, 1994). The merits of hearing directly from children who have been abused are that authentic information about the process of victimization can be obtained (Berliner and Conte, 1990; Black and Ponirakis, 2000). While indirect methods of obtaining information about child abuse (through review of official records, adult recall or parent reports) have contributed to the field, these do not offer precise estimates of the prevalence of abuse nor of the associated effects (Amaya-Jackson *et al.*, 2000, p.725). In their research, Butler *et al.* clarify that children's experiences of divorce needed to be understood, respected and valued in their own right on the basis that 'they are also often the only reliable witnesses of their own experience' (Butler *et al.*, 2003, p.10).

This book is about child abuse and presents the views of children who have been abused. The research we report on encouraged children to speak for themselves about their experiences of victimization, and to evaluate the help offered to them by professionals mandated to ensure their protection and recovery. It also aimed to make a contribution to the understanding of the impact of abuse as described by children and to emphasize the need for Australian research that treats children as legitimate users of welfare services. Marshall (1997, p.110) states:

> [I]f children are truly to be regarded as human beings and citizens in their own right, the professionals who provide the framework within which that system operates must become accustomed to considering children of all ages as consumers and clients.

Values, beliefs and orientation

Our increasing concern for and interest in how children who have experienced abuse have been silenced, as well as our growing respect for their insights and ability to move on in their lives against overwhelming odds, has had a major impact on our attitude, values and responses to children. Our professional associations, and our involvement with organizations whose main focus is on children's rights and advocacy for and on behalf of children who have been abused, has further promoted a child-centred orientation to our work and interaction with children. This approach has formed the basis for involving children who have been abused in this study and is reported on more fully in Chapter 3.

Ethical issues

In deciding to undertake research with children who have been abused and to elicit information directly from them, many major ethical concerns arose about how to ask these children about their views on their experiences of the abuse and the resultant interventions. Balancing our belief in children's rights to be heard with the need to protect them from further harm were our foremost considerations. For this reason, we have devoted a whole chapter, Chapter 4, to providing a full discussion of our ethical preoccupations and how these were considered and addressed in our research.

Definitions and terminology

The book is about children who have been abused. The definition of abuse is a complex issue. There is no agreement on a definition of child abuse and many researchers and practitioners have explored the difficulties related to a common definition of child abuse (Ammerman and Hersen, 1990; Corby, 1993; Kenward and Hevey, 1992; Zuravin, 1991). Goddard states that child abuse is used as an umbrella term to describe 'a broad range of behaviours' (1996, p.28). Some authors place the responsibility for abuse directly onto parents or those who are responsible for the care of children (see, for example, Angus and Wilkinson, 1993; Doyle, 1997a). Others draw atten-tion to the role of society and culture in sanctioning forms of abuse – for example, violence in the home (Corby, 1993; Gil, 1975; Korbin, 1987; Perry, 1996).

It is not our intention to enter into a detailed discussion on defining child abuse. However, the language we use is important and can further dis-enfranchise children as we discuss in Chapter 2. The primary objective of this book is to present how children defined and explained their abusive ex-periences. No one definition formed the basis of this study as this may have precluded some children's descriptions and experiences of abuse. There are four major forms of abuse that are commonly identified; these are physical, sexual, emotional and neglect (Browne, 1995). This method of categoriza-tion has a number of disadvantages: it does not take into account the most important dimension, the impact of the abuse and neglect on the child victim (Stanley and Goddard, 2002). Family violence or domestic violence, while evident in families for centuries, is only now being recognized as a major form of child abuse (James, 1994; Tomison, 2000). All the variables that contribute to the occurrence of child abuse need to be borne in mind as a context for understanding children's experiences of abuse.

The children who participated in the study were drawn from a children's therapy centre, an agency that specializes in providing treatment to children and young people who are victims of abuse. All the children had been assessed as victims of abuse by the child protection services and/or the police (that is, the abuse had been substantiated). Recruiting of the sample is explained further in Chapter 5.

We identify the source of each quotation by gender and age. Although all the children chose pseudonyms for themselves and were quite happy for these to be used openly, we have chosen instead a neutral method of identification largely to provide further protection for the children who participated in our research. Chapter 9, however, refers to the two participants by their chosen pseudonyms, for reasons of ease as well as relevance.

The terms 'child' and 'children' are used throughout this book to refer to all participants irrespective of their age, and include young people as well. Some researchers choose such language for a particular reason. For example, Butler *et al.* (2003) believe that gradations of childhood perpetuate the notion that childhood is defined by age alone. Our decision, however, was made out of convenience so that the language did not become cumbersome (McGee, 2000). This does not in any way reflect our attitude, approach and response to children and young people, nor how children and young people may perceive themselves.

The term 'parent' is used to refer to the person(s) who had primary responsibility for the care of the children at the time of the research. All were the non-offending parents of the children and had also been involved in the children's therapy.

The organization of the book

We begin with Chapter 2, which traces the history of how children who have been abused have been silenced. Chapter 3 explores the child-centred approach that formed the foundation for our study, and that we believe is central to any research involving children. Chapter 4, as noted above, is concerned with the ethics of undertaking research with children who have been abused as this is a major concern in any research involving abused children – especially ensuring that children are not further traumatized by the research process. The ethical issues and how these were addressed in the research process are presented in this chapter. The rationale for choosing a qualitative methodology as the most appropriate approach for this type of research is discussed in Chapter 5. Chapters 6, 7 and 8 present the voices of the children in the form of direct quotes from the research interviews. Each of these chapters reports on children's descriptions of various issues: for example, their experiences of abuse and its impact (Chapter 6); talking about the abuse, as well as their views of abusers and non-offending parents (Chapter 7); and their views on professional interventions (Chapter 8). Chapter 9 looks at children's vulnerability to abuse, and their helplessness in attempting to avoid and/or escape abuse, in the context of the experiences of two of the research participants. It compares these children's experiences with those of hostages held by terrorists. The issue of children's vulnerability to abuse is further analysed in Chapter 10 by examining factors in society that predispose children to abuse. Chapter 11 explores the complex issue of listening to children and what this might mean in practical terms. In conclusion, Chapter 12 reviews the important messages about abuse that emerged from talking with children who have been abused.

CHAPTER 2

The Silencing of Children

The courts didn't listen to me when I was young. You know, little do they know what happened to me. You know, it's sort of unfair when you think about it...

13-year-old male

This chapter forms the historical foundation for the research that follows. Readers are warned that this chapter includes court proceedings related to details of rape and severe abuse to children that may prove to be distresssng.

Introduction: the invisible child

The reader of history with an interest in children and childhood is likely to gain two significant impressions: first, that children do not feature very prominently in historical texts; and, second, it is clear that children have a very long history of suffering at the hands of adults (Goddard, 1996). One explanation for the absence of children from these historical accounts is proposed by Ariès (1962), who suggests that children rarely appear in historical sources because childhood was not viewed as a separate stage of human development.

Childhood, in other words, is described as a 'recent invention' (Goddard, 1996, p.7). Jenks (1996, p.62) suggests that Ariès is describing a time when 'children were invisible...what Ariès is illuminating is that the manner of their recognition by adults...the forms of their relationships with adults, [have] altered through the passage of time'.

Jenks goes on to propose that this view is easier to understand when we reflect upon the comparatively 'recent invention of the "youth", "adolescent" or "teenager"', a group that has been recognized only since the Second World War (1996, p.63).

Archard (1993), in a review of Ariès' argument that the concept of child-hood did not emerge until the late seventeenth century, describes the publi-cation of the work as coming at a particularly important time. Intellectual and political pressures combined to subject childhood to far greater scrutiny. The change has been 'recent and dramatic'. 'Even in comparatively recent times, children were ignored, or referred to only indirectly, in histories' (Goddard, 1996, p.8).

Goddard points out that Manning Clark's *A Short History of Australia* (1986), for example, makes little direct reference to children: 'Children are present to be sure, but largely in the form of histories of institutions and services, and not in their own right' (Goddard, 1996, p.8).

Although children may have been 'invisible', what is now known as child abuse has always existed. Radbill (1980), for example, outlines a cata-logue of horrors against children throughout history: child labour, exposure, infanticide and child sexual abuse, among others.

It is our contention that these abusive acts against children have contin-ued, in part at least, because children were not only 'invisible' but also rendered inaudible. The 'invisible' child may have become more visible but has remained to a large extent inaudible. A number of factors have contrib-uted to the silencing of the child who has been abused.

Even the screams are silenced: the modern 'discovery' of child abuse

It is now generally accepted that the work of Dr Henry Kempe and his col-leagues created modern interest in child abuse. Their article (Kempe *et al.*, 1962), published in the *Journal of the American Medical Association*, has been granted the position of seminal work in this area. Entitled 'The Battered-child Syndrome', the work caused widespread interest in the problem, not only in the USA but also in the UK and Australia (Goddard and Carew, 1993).

Kempe *et al.*'s paper reported on a nationwide survey in the USA that was designed to establish the incidence of the problem. Some 71 hospitals replied, reporting 302 cases. Eighty-five of the children were described as suffering 'permanent brain injury' and 33 of the children died (Kempe *et al.*, 1962). Kempe and his fellow researchers reported that in a third of the cases 'proper medical diagnosis' led to legal action. The researchers also surveyed 77 district attorneys, who reported that 'they had knowledge of 447 cases in a similar one-year period' (1962, p.17). Of these, 29 suffered 'permanent brain damage' and 45 died. Legal action in these cases was taken in 46 per cent of cases (1962, p.17).

Kempe *et al.*'s work was followed by similar research elsewhere. The first such article in the Australian literature (Storey, 1964), however, drew on cases from the UK and USA and was in fact written in the latter. Storey stated that this was because 'no cases have been reported in the Australian literature' (1964, p.789).

In fact, this was not the whole story. As has been noted elsewhere (Goddard, 1981), reference was made to what is now known as child abuse far earlier. In his history of child health and welfare in Australia, Gandevia (1978, p.103), for example, notes that 'the "battered baby syndrome" is likely to be as old as civilization'. Gandevia's research shows that 'infanticide' was a major concern a century or so earlier, in 1863, when 'in about 25% of inquests on children under 3 years of age death could be attributed to causes denoting neglect, ignorance or maltreatment' (1978, p.104).

Gandevia suggested that this pattern continued into the 1870s but juries were 'reluctant to bring a verdict of infanticide against mothers' (1978, p.104). In 1964, Storey started his article by describing 'the battered-child syndrome' as an 'abhorrent entity' (1964, p.789).

The following year, an article appeared in the *Australian Paediatric Journal* based on cases at the Adelaide Children's Hospital (Wurfel and Maxwell, 1965). Twenty-six children were studied from 18 families drawn from the hospital over ten years. Eight of the children died as a result of their injuries. It is extraordinary to note that Wurfel and Maxwell state that 'sporadic accounts of such episodes are commonly found in the Australian lay-press' but that, in spite of this coverage in the media, there had been 'no examination of the problem in Australian medical literature' (1965, p.127).

The Medical Journal of Australia (10 December 1966) followed up this work with an editorial and two further articles. While Storey (1964) referred to the 'battered child' and Wurfel and Maxwell (1965) the 'battered child syndrome', the articles in this issue were devoted to 'neglected babies' (Bialestock, 1966) and the 'maltreatment syndrome' (Birrell and Birrell, 1966).

Birrell and Birrell described eight cases of child abuse that came to police attention. Two deaths occurred and the authors suggested that 'the blind application of the "philosophy" that even a bad home is better than no home or the best possible institution' caused those deaths (Birrell and Birrell, 1966, p.1137).

Bialestock's (1966) paper was particularly interesting and prescient, and broke new ground in describing what Gil (1975) would describe as the three levels of child abuse: abusive conditions in the home, and abusive interactions between caregivers and children; the institutional level of abuse; and the societal level where social policies sanction or cause deficits in child development. Again, it should be noted, however, that the term 'neglected babies' used by Bialestock is somewhat euphemistic as it is stated that many had minor abrasions and bruises, and that limb and skull fractures were not rare (Goddard, 1981).

It is interesting to reflect upon these papers from the perspective of the child. At first glance, the children may be said to be central to the research and in one sense they are. The papers describe horrendous abuse in graphic detail. Kempe *et al.*'s paper contains 'radiologic features' with several X-rays of injured children. The paper by Birrell and Birrell (1966) is far more graphic, with photographs of the children themselves.

Kempe *et al.*'s paper is concerned with the 'battered-child syndrome' as a 'clinical condition'; it seeks to describe the 'clinical manifestations' (1962, p.17). The paper describes the 'emotional unwillingness' of doctors 'to consider abuse as the cause of the child's difficulty' (1962, p.18). Doctors are also described as unfamiliar with the healing of fractures and so they are uncertain as to 'the significance of the lesions that are present' (p.18). The paper is illustrated with X-rays because, as the researchers state, 'To the informed physician, the bones tell a story the child is too young or frightened to tell' (Kempe *et al.*, 1962, p.18).

The absence of children's voices appears understandable, given that Kempe and his colleagues state that while the clinical condition they are describing, 'the battered-child syndrome', can 'occur at any age…in general, the affected children are younger than 3 years' (1962, p.17).

It is too easy to assume, however, that the children were too young to tell of their experiences. Birrell and Birrell describe each of their cases in some detail, and each one is assigned a separate number. Although the children were in general very young, Case 7 describes a nine-year-old child who was:

> kept tied hand and foot for two days in a shed during extremely hot weather. She was strapped with a razor strap and fed only dry bread and water. Her father maintained that she was a wicked girl, and kept an incredible diary of her alleged misdoings and his punishments. (Birrell and Birrel, 1966, p.1136)

It is Case 5 in this paper that is particularly poignant. There are two photographs of the subject, a girl aged three years, in the article. One shows her from the waist up, head tilted to one side, showing 'bruising of body, arms and face, with lacerations'. The other photograph is a rear view, body length, and an adult hand is seen holding the girl's hand; this shows 'multiple bruises of various ages on back, thigh, legs and arms' together with 'strap marks' (Birrell and Birrell, 1966, p.1136).

The photographs, terrible though they are, do not adequately describe the full horror of this young girl's life:

> [The photographs] show a girl, aged three years, with multiple bruises of varying ages. The father had separated from the mother when the child was aged 10 months, and had come to live in a country town, boarding with a woman with five children who looked after his child. The woman observed the child being strapped several times with his belt, and noticed when bathing the child that there were red marks on the back and shoulders and that the child had a painful left arm. The woman took her to hospital, where x-ray films showed no abnormalities... The child was in hospital for 10 days, where she screamed and ran from the father whenever he visited.

Even the screams of this young child were in vain. She was returned home. She had effectively been rendered inaudible:

> The child was nevertheless returned to the father, well and without a mark, but in fear of him. She would not speak to him. Because of this, at 5 o'clock every night after work he thrashed her with his belt after undressing her. Finally, during a drinking bout, he hit the landlady when she remonstrated with him for hitting the child across the face, strapping her on the back and legs and dropping her on the floor. Police were called... Her cheeks were so bruised she could not chew. Her body was a mass of bruises of varying stages, the skin being broken in a number of places. (Birrell and Birrell, 1966, p.1135)

Child deaths

The report of the United States Advisory Board on Child Abuse and Neglect (1995), entitled *A Nation's Shame*, is based on a two-year study of child fatalities. The report draws the conclusion that 'luck plays a major role' in deciding which children survive serious physical abuse and which do not (1995, p.17). In the UK, Sanders states that it is 'almost impossible to overestimate' the influence of child abuse deaths on child protection systems (1999, p.160).

The names of the children in question are well known to those working in health and social care in the UK. They include Susan Auckland, Tyra Henry, Kimberley Carlile and Maria Colwell (see, for example, Stanley and Goddard, 2002).

In Australia, the child abuse death that had the greatest effect was the murder of Daniel Valerio. The murder trial, and the subsequent coronial inquest, attracted media attention throughout Australia. The headlines (see, for example, 'Fatal Inaction', Weekes, 1994) both reflected and stirred public outrage at Daniel's brutal death and at the apparent inability of no fewer than 20 professionals to prevent it (Goddard, 1996).

Daniel's life and death has been described in detail elsewhere (see, for example, Goddard, 1996, pp.173–83). A brief synopsis is provided here, based on the report of the State Coroner, the internal inquiry report of protective services, and media coverage (Goddard and Liddell, 1995).

Daniel was born in 1988 to Michael Valerio and Cheryl Butcher. He was Cheryl's fourth child, her second by Michael Valerio. Her relationship with Valerio ended in 1989; she met Paul Aiton early in 1990 and he soon moved into her home. A neighbour reported that she often saw Daniel and his brother with bruising and heard the cries of children coming from the house. The neighbour said that the cries sounded as if the children were being beaten. From June 1990, a number of other people, including three doctors and a teacher, saw bruising on Daniel.

Early in June, a general practitioner saw bruising to Daniel's head and face. Cheryl explained that this was due to a fall and gave the same explanation to a teacher. In July, Cheryl took Daniel to another GP because the child had a bump on the back of his head. The GP noted bruises around Daniel's eyes and forehead. The GP reported that there was no adequate explanation. Less than a week later, another GP in the same medical centre saw a large haematoma on Daniel's forehead. Again there was no adequate explanation.

A paediatrician then saw Daniel, and he noted a significant number of bruises to the boy's body, head and limbs. He arranged hospital admission. Daniel did well in hospital, put on weight, and was described as affectionate towards staff. No new bruises appeared while he was in hospital but it was decided that there were insufficient grounds to refer to protective services. A follow-up appointment was made for nearly four weeks later for Daniel to be reviewed by the paediatrician but Daniel and his mother failed to attend.

The day after hospital discharge, Cheryl, Daniel and his brother saw a community health worker who saw bruising on Daniel's face. A few days later, the same worker saw bruises to Daniel's legs. Daniel's brother did not attend this appointment as his mother reported that he had suffered a fractured clavicle (collar bone).

Soon afterwards, Paul Aiton, Cheryl Butcher and the three children (the fourth was living in Queensland) moved into another house. An anonymous call was made to protective services expressing concern that Paul Aiton was abusing Daniel. A week later an electrician working in the house called the police because of bruising to Daniel's face and limbs. The next day another anonymous call was made to protective services.

At about the same time, on 30 August, the police were visiting the house where Cheryl Butcher and Daniel's four-year-old brother were present. The police saw bruising on the boy's face and limbs. The boy said that the bruising was caused by a fall, by being hit with a stick on his legs by Paul Aiton, and by being smacked by his mother. The boy went and got the tree branch that he said Aiton had used to hit him.

The same day, Cheryl Butcher took Daniel and his brother to the GP who had seen Daniel in June. He noted bruising to Daniel's head, trunk and abdomen, and to his brother's face and abdomen. He contacted the paediatrician but contacted neither the police nor protective services. Later that day, the police revisited the house and found bruising to Daniel's head, chest, back, groin and legs. Paul Aiton denied using the tree branch. The next day a part-time police surgeon took photographs of the bruising to both boys.

On 5 September, Cheryl took Daniel back to the GP who had seen him most recently, seeking advice about his continual vomiting. The GP noted multiple bruising to Daniel's head, trunk and abdomen. The next day, the same GP saw Daniel again. He presented with persistent vomiting, tender stomach, raised temperature and diarrhoea. Gastroenteritis was diagnosed. The following day, 7 September, the GP reviewed Daniel. On 8 September he was finally beaten to death by Paul Aiton.

The post-mortem revealed 104 bruises all over Daniel's body. Severe internal injuries were found, akin to the crushing trauma found in road accident victims. These had resulted in severe haemorrhaging, the cause of death. There was a suggestion of earlier abdominal trauma. In addition, there were healing fractures of both collarbones.

As has been observed elsewhere, similar mistakes and omissions have been found in many inquiries into child abuse deaths around the world: poor management; staff shortages; the failure to follow procedures; inadequate recording; role confusion; and failure to communicate (Goddard, 1996). All were present in Daniel Valerio's death.

Closer analysis of the death of Daniel Valerio reveals two other important issues. The first came from the mouth of Daniel's brother. He reported that he had been beaten with a stick. He took the police to retrieve the weapon. He identified the assailant. He even pointed out the injuries. This scene took place in the home. If the crime had occurred elsewhere, and the child had been assaulted by a stranger, the responses of the system may have been completely different (Goddard, 1996). As it was, the report of abuse by a child in his home was apparently inaudible.

The second prompted the research into language (discussed below). As is often the case, the examination of Daniel Valerio's death lasted longer than his life (see, for example, Goddard and Tucci, 2004). The coronial inquest revealed a great deal about the place of children in our society. Although Daniel's brother was able to report the abuse, Daniel himself had mastered few words. Among his limited repertoire, the court was told, was the word 'hurt', such a short, sharp word from such a small boy about such large injuries. Others in the proceedings were less precise: phrases such as 'its parents' rather than 'his parents' passed unnoticed (Goddard, 1993).

There have been a number of criticisms of child death inquiries. Stanley and Goddard (2002), for example, strongly criticize the failure of inquiries and researchers (for example, Reder, Duncan and Gray, 1993) to examine fully other violence occurring in and around the families and the possible effects on those that seek to intervene.

We must also consider the position children hold in our society. For child abuse to be appropriately responded to, children have to be regarded as 'more than objects' – they have to be 'viewed as individuals who have rights of their own and needs for special protection' (Goddard, 1993, p.11).

In the UK, more recently, the murder of eight-year-old Victoria Climbié in 2000 exposed major problems in the child protection services responsible for her welfare. Victoria had been brought to Europe from West Africa, and died of hypothermia after months of torture inflicted by her great-aunt and the great-aunt's boyfriend (Lord Laming, 2003).

In a paper that focuses on comparing the inquiry reports into the deaths, some 30 years apart, of Maria Colwell and Victoria Climbié, Parton (2004) commences by identifying some of the similarities: the awful injuries and neglect suffered by both; the lack of appropriate intervention; the inadequacies of the child protection systems; and the poor communication and recording. Buried among the lists is what we regard as an issue absolutely central to the horrendous deaths of Maria Colwell and Victoria Climbié: 'considerable failure to engage and communicate directly with the children themselves about their feelings and circumstances' (Parton, 2004, p.82).

The failure to talk to and listen to these children casts a long shadow over their lives and deaths, just as happened in the case of Daniel Valerio. As was noted more forcefully elsewhere: 'The most chilling sentence in the report into the death of Victoria Climbié refers to the eight-year-old shouting at a social worker: "I am not lying. I must tell you more. It is true"' (Womack, 2003). This 'outburst' from a child who was usually 'quiet' and 'nervous' was Victoria's attempt to tell professionals what was happening to her (Womack, 2003).

'It's always – always going to be in my head': a case of repeated abuse

This part of the chapter is largely based on an article, 'A Case of Repeated Abuse' by Chris Goddard (2000), which appeared in *The Age* newspaper. The article carried the following subheading: *'Warning: readers may be offended by parts of this article. It includes court proceedings relating to rape.'* We reiterate this caution here.

Child abuse, as we have seen, is not only committed by adults, it is defined by them too. The responses of adults, as we have seen, can make things better or worse for the child who has been abused (Goddard, 2000). Children who have been badly hurt can get badly hurt again as adults respond. Adults can make it extremely difficult and painful for children to tell of their abuse.

This is the story of a young woman (referred to as AB in the proceedings), aged 17 years, who appeared in the Supreme Court in Victoria, Australia, in 2000. There are similar cases from around the world. She was awarded A\$490,000 (around £200,000) in damages by a Supreme Court jury. The Court found that the primary school AB attended should have acted upon the warning signs that she was being sexually abused. In short, the school failed in its duty of care to a girl in Grade Three, aged nine years.

The most distressing lesson of AB's story is almost too painful to relate. For anything resembling justice to be done, AB had to tell her story over and over again. She had told her mother, her father and the police. She had been cross-examined in a committal hearing. She had been further cross-examined in the trial of her stepfather, who was found guilty of repeatedly raping her (he spent only three years in jail). Then, in the Victoria Supreme Court, AB suffered what one prays will be the final assault. She was cross-examined by her stepfather, the man who raped her. He chose to represent himself and was allowed to further traumatize his victim, this time in front of a jury.

AB was allowed some protection – some of her evidence-in-chief was given through an affidavit, and she was cross-examined by the rapist through audio-visual link from a remote witness room in a nearby building – but both shields provided inadequate protection.

By the time her stepfather started his cross-examination, AB had already been taken through 'incidents' of rape, of beatings that were worse when her mother wasn't there, of disregarded intervention orders. She had lost contact with her grandmother and her half-sister. She had even lost contact with her mother; the day her stepfather was sentenced was the last time she talked to her mother.

In the court, AB was asked by Jeremy Ruskin, QC, senior counsel for the state, if she would feel better once this case was over. She replied, 'It's always – always going to be in my head, it's always – it's never going to go away and this court case is relating to the actual abuse, so the court case is always going to be there as well.'

Then her stepfather began. His first question was:

> 'Your evidence…refers to pain in your vagina, right?'
> 'Yes.'
> 'In your first statement, you said it was up and down for a long time, right, you remember that?'
> 'Yes.'
> 'Do you recall saying that I inserted my penis into your vagina, do you remember that…no?'
> 'Yes, I do.'
> 'And then you said it seemed for a long time up and down, is that right?'
> 'Yes that's correct.'

And so it goes on. A convicted rapist, seven or eight years later, is cross-examining his victim, who was nine or ten at the time of the rapes. There are questions about whether there was blood, about who checked the sheets. It is hard to understand how any of this is necessary, how it might be relevant when he has already been convicted.

'You say that I forced your legs apart…right?' The stepfather then reads from one of the statements the girl had made years earlier: 'I can remember him walking over…drawing the curtains…pulling down my pants…'. He attempts to suggest there are contradictions in her statements.

> AB: 'I don't know which paragraph to look at because you are not telling me…'
>
> [The stepfather persists:] 'You say…that "I was on my stomach and [he] pushed my legs apart by grabbing my knees at the back…"'
>
> [And he persists:] 'If you look at one statement, and look at the other statement, one statement is very blunt, right, is very plain, but the other statement is more graphic…?'

After some explanation, AB replies: 'I'll knock your f—ing block off.' The judge, Bill Gillard, interjects. To AB he says 'just, please, listen to the question', and to the stepfather, 'You cross-examine as you see fit.'

The stepfather says he is lost. The judge advises him:

> If you seek to show there is a difference between the two statements, you first of all refer to the first statement, draw [her] attention to the parts you're dealing with, ask her to read that and then ask her to read the similar paragraph in the second statement involving the same incident, if you wish to highlight there is a difference.

And still it goes on. The stepfather, convicted of rape, talks of 'allegations'. In response to this insult, AB threatens to come into the court and 'f—ing rip your neck off your shoulders'; 'Every question you ask…it takes you ten…minutes to ask it, obviously you don't know what you are talking about…'.

At one point counsel for the victim intercedes: 'I think the jury are a little bit distressed.' Later, Justice Gillard says to AB, 'I do ask you to listen to the question and answer it, and stay calm. I think we all appreciate the ordeal, but I can assure you the whole procedure will go a lot quicker if you just listen to the question and answer it to the best of your ability.'

She asks if her stepfather can be made to ask his questions more quickly. The stepfather asks questions about 'the secret'. He suggests she had a 'secret' with her natural father: 'Did you do this…?'; 'So you totally deny this…?'; 'I am stating to you…'.

The words 'Witness distressed' appear in the transcript. It goes on.

> Justice Gillard: 'All right, now come on…please.' (Witness distressed.)

> AB: 'You're telling me to come on, and you're letting this arse-wipe cross-examine me and I'm not even in the court room to smash him. Don't give me that shit.'

And later:

> Justice Gillard: 'Look, this is getting a bit out of hand...'. (Witness distressed.)
> AB: 'Well you guys are the ones that wanted him to cross-examine me, not me – not me...'

In Britain, a series of much-publicized rape trials has led to a ban on rape defendants, rather than their lawyers, cross-examining their alleged victims. In one case, the victim was questioned for six days about the details of her 16-hour rape ordeal. The rapist wore the same clothes he had worn when he assaulted her.

The victim later spoke about the case in the hope that other women would be spared such experiences: 'I feel that I have been raped twice, once in his filthy den and once in front of a judge and jury... When a rapist is asking the questions, he knows what he has done, and is furthering the act,' she said.

AB's case was a truly shocking example of how cruelly children can be treated. It was a civil case, not a criminal trial involving life and liberty. Her stepfather had already been convicted of repeatedly raping her when she was a child. Even now, AB is barely more than a child.

In researching AB's case, the full transcript of the proceedings was obtained from the court transcription service. The full horror of the case had also had its effects on those whose job it was to word-process the full proceedings. We were told that, rather than one person transcribing the whole case, the typists had to take it in turns to transcribe the full cross-examination as they found it so distressing.

In an extraordinary coincidence, as we were putting the finishing touches to this book, the case of AB and the brutality of her cross-examination were revisited by Australian newspapers in the light of plans to introduce new laws to protect sexual abuse victims in the legal system (Ellingsen, 2005). This led to further reports of children traumatized by their treatment in court. In one case, it was reported that a 16-year-old girl tried to commit suicide after a judge ordered her to justify, in front of her father, why she did not want to testify in his presence. The father faces incest charges against her and her brother aged 14 years (Butcher, 2005).

The use of language to minimize the harm to children

As we noted above, according to Gandevia (1978), there was media concern about child deaths in the mid-nineteenth century. The relationship between child abuse and the media is a long and complex one (Goddard and Liddell, 1995), and media representations of child abuse have themselves become an important area of study (see, for example, the 'Special Issue' of *Child Abuse Review*, 1996).

As we have seen, it was media attention that allowed Kempe *et al.*'s (1962) study to be granted the seminal status it is now accorded, largely ignoring the earlier work that radiologists and social workers had carried out (Howitt, 1992). According to Nelson (1984, p.54), media attention has transformed a 'once-minor charity concern called "cruelty to children" into an important social issue'. It is Nelson's argument that the media not only responded to the problem of child abuse but also, in part at least, 'created' it and the public's sense that there was an urgent need to respond to it.

A great deal of the scholarly analysis of child abuse has been concerned with the 'unevenness' of journalists' reporting (Franklin and Parton, 1991, p.9), but until recently very little attention has been paid to scrutiny of the language used to describe child abuse and the children who are victims of abuse in the media texts. Goddard and Saunders (2000) have suggested that the failure to closely analyse the language used may be due to the complexity of the area. Discourse analysis involves a number of disciplines, including sociology, social and cognitive psychology, philosophy and literary studies.

They point out that the importance of the language used to describe and represent social issues has been widely recognized in other fields. Language has been described as a major issue for feminists (Cameron, 1990), and the sexist features of language have been widely documented – for example, the generic use of 'he' and 'man' (Fairclough, 1992, p.21). Benedict argues that myths about rape are perpetuated by gender bias in language (1992).

Fairclough (1995) states that textual analysis should play an important role in all social science research, citing four major reasons: theoretical, methodological, political and historical. In theoretical terms, texts are part of social action; he states that 'the language is widely misperceived as transparent, so that [the] social and ideological "work" that language does in producing, reproducing or transforming social structures, relations and identities is routinely "overlooked"' (pp.208–9).

In methodological terms, texts can provide evidence about social structures, processes and relationships. Evidence of social change can be provided through historical analysis. In political terms, social control and domination are exercised through texts (Fairclough, 1995).

These are the reasons why the examination of the coverage of child abuse cases in the media is important. Research at Monash University into coverage in the English language has noted a number of features that are relevant to the status of children.

- *The child may be called 'it'.* The use of the pronoun 'it' for a child is common. While this probably avoids the awkward use of 'he or she' (Goddard and Saunders, 2000, p.41), analysis of the media has shown that 'he or she' is used when representing adults.

- *The child may become 'it'.* In some circumstances, the gender of a child who has been abused, or who is at risk of abuse, is identified and then lost as the story unfolds. The child becomes 'it'. This 'gender slippage' or 'gender neglect' is confined to stories where children are abused, neglected or are described as at risk (Goddard and Saunders, 2000, pp.40–3). No other examples of this loss of gender were found in other stories. Goddard and Saunders reviewed the work of Wales, who suggests that the use of 'it' for a baby or infant may be acceptable on the grounds that the baby is not yet born, that the sex is not known, or that babies 'lack reason or speech' (1996, p.159). They note that Wales (1996, p.160) cautions that the use of the word 'it' may also signify 'lack of emotional involvement'. Goddard and Saunders suggest that this 'gender slippage' may be 'an emotional perhaps unconscious, response' to the unpleasant nature of child abuse (2000, p.43).

- *The seriousness of child sexual abuse is reduced by the language used.* Goddard and Saunders show that child sexual abuse may be redefined as 'a less serious, almost consensual relationship between adults' (2000, p.44). Among the examples cited is the case of a man jailed for seven years for the repeated sexual assault of his ten-year-old stepdaughter. The girl became pregnant at the age of 11. Newspaper reports described this as 'an affair', and the perpetrator and victim were described as 'the couple' (2000, p.43).

Goddard and Saunders (2000) describe this rewriting of offences against children as 'textual abuse', an approach that allows the writer or reader to distance him or herself from the abuse being described: 'Textual abuse is an umbrella term that includes: language that objectifies children; language that reframes and minimises the seriousness of offences against children; language that exploits children and language that degrades children and denies their gender' (Saunders and Goddard, 2001, p.446).

This language analysis has been extended to examine so-called 'child prostitution', where those who commit sexual offences against children are redefined as 'customers' and 'clients', and the offence itself is transformed through language into a commercial transaction or a form of employment (Goddard *et al.*, 2005).

Although this analysis commenced with the print media, it has been extended to a broader range of literature (see Goddard and Saunders, 2000). 'Textual abuse' of children has been found in a wide range of literature across a range of disciplines, including medicine, law, sociology, psychology, anthropology, history and social work (Saunders and Goddard, 2001). Of particular significance, Saunders and Goddard describe examples in journal articles and books primarily concerned with children's rights, child abuse and even the 'new childhood studies' (2001, p.447).

This is particularly ironic, given that the international children's rights documents perfectly illustrate a progression in the use of personal pronouns chosen by the children's rights advocates to refer to a child: in the 1924 Declaration of the Rights of the Child, the child is referred to as 'it'; in the 1959 version, the child is identified by the generic pronoun 'he'; and, in the UN Convention of the Rights of the Child in 1989, the term 'his or her' is repeatedly used (Saunders and Goddard, 2001, p.448).

Cloke and Davies argue that children's low status was emphasized by the need for a convention, children being apparently excluded from the human rights entitlements, just as 'the term "he" was supposed to incorporate "she" but in fact served...to exclude and marginalize women' (1995, p.25).

These forms of 'textual abuse', the rewriting of crimes against children, not only diminish the harm to children but also, by seeking to protect readers and writers, ensure that children's rights and children's pain are not fully acknowledged (Saunders and Goddard, 2001). Through 'textual' abuse, language perpetuates the low status of children and the lack of respect given to their rights. Saunders and Goddard argue that we must be critically aware of 'the power of language to influence how children are regarded and treated' (2001, p.458).

Saunders (2005) argues that language is used to minimize the seriousness of 'physical punishment' of children. It can indeed be the 'rapist's camouflage' (Goddard *et al.*, 2005). Language contributes to the inferior status of

children which, for example, 'permits and condones violent and hurtful responses to a child' that would not be tolerated as a response to adults
(Saunders and Goddard, 2005, p.113). Language, however, is but one part of
society's construction of childhood, and there have been and are other forces
at work to silence children.

Other forces that silence children

As we have seen, the silencing of children has a long and effective history. In
child sexual abuse, a number of writers (for example, Rush, 1980) have suggested that Sigmund Freud changed his view that sexual trauma in childhood quite commonly occurred and could cause major problems later in life.
This view caused considerable hostility in his colleagues and Freud adopted
the more acceptable proposition that child sexual abuse was the product of
fantasy (see, for example, Goddard and Carew, 1993).

Some 50 years ago, Kinsey and his colleagues (1953) also contributed to
the silencing of children. They acknowledged that the problem of sexual
abuse was widespread, but suggested that serious consequences were exag-
gerated (Goddard and Carew, 1993). A number of myths were used to
minimize the problem: children were said to lie about sexual abuse; they
were said to fantasize about sexual abuse; children were said to be sexually
provocative or seductive; incest was said to be part of a caring relationship;
sexual abuse was said to be not harmful but intervention was; strangers were
said to be the real danger; and mothers were said to be always collusive
(Goddard and Carew, 1993).

These myths have continued to be used, particularly by organizations
seeking to protect themselves against accusations of abuse. The Catholic
Church in particular has been guilty of placing its own interests ahead
of those of children (Goddard, 2003). Other churches have also had
well-publicized failures. Only recently, Australia's Governor-General, Peter
Hollingworth (a former Anglican Archbishop), resigned after apparently
accusing a young girl of 'leading a priest on', and stating that he did not
condone a bishop's sex with a young girl 'regardless of whether or not the
girl was a willing participant' (Goddard, 2003, p.17).

The problems children who have been abused face are deep-seated and
long-standing. The responses of professionals are part of those problems and
are equally entrenched. Many of the professionals currently working with
children were trained in ways that accentuated rather than alleviated children's disadvantage. A leading casework text of the 1970s, for example, in a

section on communicating with children noted their 'limited vocabulary', their 'limited ability to conceptualise', and their 'confusion between the real and the imaginary, which makes fantasies rife and may result in telling lies' (Berry, 1972, p.46).

At the same time as learning more about child abuse and neglect, it appears that we are also discovering new ways of abusing children. Two examples illustrate this point. In Australia, the children of asylum-seekers, or other 'unauthorized' or 'illegal' arrivals, can be held in so-called detention centres for years. These prisons with electric fences and razor wire are often in hot and remote parts of the country (Liddell and Goddard, 2005, p.11). These children spend years in 'what is, in effect, a prison. Children…are compelled to watch their families divided and damaged, parental roles disintegrating' (Goddard and Briskman, 2004, p.17). Furthermore, there is now growing evidence to suggest that the globalization of child pornography and the use of the Internet are relatively new media for abusing children (see, for example, Goddard, 2004; Stanley, 2001).

Conclusion

Children and young people are rarely heard. Children who have been abused and neglected are heard even less. It is as if they are further abused and neglected by society in general, as well as by the abusive adults. The reality may be that we do not want to hear what they say because their words are too painful to absorb (Goddard and Mudaly, 2003). Children were, perhaps, invisible. They still have trouble making themselves heard. Jenks (1996) suggests that children's relationships with adults have changed. It may be that they have changed less than we like to think.

CHAPTER 3

Child-centred Practice

The Foundation of Effective Research with Children who have been Abused

You need to get people who listen, not people who are there for the money, people who want to hear the truth…and help children.

12-year-old female

Introduction

If we are to give recognition to children's views, we must find a way to listen to and hear what children think, feel and need (Milner and Carolin, 1999). For this to occur, 'society has to recognise them as real, individual human beings with rights of their own, rather than as appendages of parents who have a right to own them' (Leach, 1990, p.179). Much has now been written on the need to and how to communicate effectively with and listen to children (Bannister, Barrett and Shearer, 1990; Brock, 1993; Butler *et al.*, 2003; Christensen, 2004; Doyle, 1997a; Geldard and Geldard, 1997; Grover, 2004; Hughes, 1997, 2005; James, 1989; Jones, 1990; Mayall, 1994; Oaklander, 1997, 1988). The importance of listening to children is emphasized by Bannister *et al.* (1990, p.xv), who state that it 'is the foundation upon which we can give children their rights as people and ensure their voice is heard'.

To do this Christensen insists that children need to be accepted 'primarily as fellow human beings' (2004, p.165) rather than as 'objects of concern' (Bannister *et al.*, 1990, p.xii) or as 'research subjects' (Mullender *et al.*, 2002, p.12). Therefore when involving children in research, Christensen (2004) believes that, in principle, they should not to be treated as different from adults. She states that different research methods or ethical standards should not be assumed just because they are children. We agree with these senti-ments but believe that research with children *who have been abused* does, in fact, require special consideration and thought. Historically, writing about children who have been abused has been by adults. There is now increasing recognition of even very young children's competence to comment on their own lives and be involved in decision-making (Alderson, 1995; Sinclair, 2004). We believe that the focus should be not on representing the voices of children who have been abused but on promoting children's participation and giving them opportunities to have their own voices heard. To do so one must attempt to appreciate how the world looks from the child's perspective. If not, approaches and procedures may be adopted that may 'be insensitive, ineffective and even counter-productive. In short, we will fail children' (Bray and Pugh, 1997, p.143).

This chapter argues for and stresses the need for a child-centred approach in research and in any interventions with children who have been abused. We believe that this would demonstrate respect for childhood, the particular features that define this period of human development, and the impact of abuse on children. In the following exploration of this approach, the views of children who participated in our study are also woven into the discussion.

A child-centred approach: core components

It is our view that having a child-centred approach, which keeps children central at all times, promotes children's involvement in processes that affect them. This means that features that are specific to childhood, and integral to children's ways of experiencing their world, must form the foundation for any work with them. This is even more essential when working with children who have been abused: 'Child centred practice reflects a particular set of beliefs about the capacities, vulnerabilities and rights of children. Its core is a commitment to children's ways of understanding, describing and doing' (Australian Childhood Foundation, 2001, 2003).

In such an approach, the needs and welfare of children are the primary concern and focus of practice. The approach includes processes that shape and examine professional knowledge and practice to ensure that they promote the best interests of each child and of children generally. It also examines the impact of this knowledge and practice, and explicitly consid-ers the ideological and ethical basis on which decisions regarding children are made (Gilligan, 1994). The effectiveness of interventions must be examined in terms of outcomes for children, rather than for professionals, parents, family or agency. Goddard (1996) is critical of how the specific needs of children who have been harmed by abuse and neglect are disregarded in professional interventions: 'The emphasis appears to be on making the child fit into the services, rather than ensuring services to those in need' (Goddard, 1996, p.186).

A child-centred approach, on the other hand, focuses on the child's potential for growth rather than the child's problem (Webb, 1996). To develop such an approach requires a child-centred belief system. This involves understanding our current beliefs about children, comprehending our own experiences of childhood, of being parents, and acknowledging the social, cultural and organizational contextual belief system within which we work (Gilligan, 1994). It requires us to accept that our personal and professional belief system has a significant impact on our work.

Particular features that define childhood and promote children's participation in research and interventions with them include those described below.

The environment

Child-centred environments need to be attractive and welcoming to the child without being pretentious and too sophisticated. They must be accessible and appropriate for children (Ross, 1990) and have a 'warm and comfortable feel about [them], as distinct from the ambience of most clinical rooms...' (Geldard and Geldard, 1997, p.85). It is preferable that the same room be used every time a child is seen in order to set the child at ease immediately and promote a sense of belonging.

An 11-year-old girl who participated in our research talks about her experience of being interviewed by the police and how the environment has an impact on children's responses:

> Both times in the office, one was under, um, video camera and the other time was just on paper. The first time it wasn't as scary because we were in a sort of brightly coloured room and there were all stuffed toys around. But the next time, there was this grey room with nothing there...and just the video camera and everything and it was harder to think. This wasn't in the brightly coloured room for some reason because that was sort of a more happy sort of room... (11-year-old female)

The person working with the child

The professionals involved with the child need to have 'a clear idea of the needs and rights of children and of the stages of normal development' (Calam and Franchi, 1987, p.195). The person must be skilled and knowledgeable about communicating with children at their developmental level (Atwool, 2000). They must be comfortable to engage in play with the child. He/she must convey a genuine respect for the child, be able to communicate verbally and non-verbally, and ensure that the therapeutic environment is safe (Smedley, 1999). In addition the person must have a wide range of techniques at his/her disposal, a clear theoretical foundation and a commitment in terms of both time and energy (James, 1989). The importance of this is conveyed in the following quote:

> I had two [counsellors]; one before that was very, didn't know nothing. She just didn't know much about counselling and all that. We'd talk about it and then she'd [say], righto, see you tomorrow, something like that. (11-year-old male)

Play

Play is an important consideration (Oaklander, 1997; Webb, 1996) as it is the 'child's preferred and natural medium of expression' (Schaefer and Cangelosi, 1993, p.4). In such play, the child is treated as an equal and his or her opinions and views are respected and listened to attentively. Even teenagers traumatized by abusive experiences appreciate the diversion that games, drawing and play material offer when addressing their pain (Smedley, 1999). The following quotes confirm this.

> …and just play the games, and, talk for about twenty minutes and that's the way to do it. (11-year-old male)

> It's good, like, to have fun… Because, like, if you just explain it [talk about the abuse] just sitting there it's really hard… Sometimes I coloured in stuff, played games. (13-year-old male)

> Well, it was really comforting because I can draw or play games and stuff like that… (11-year-old female)

> Yeah. I think you need bits and pieces, it can sort of get a bit much if you're just sitting around all the time talking and talking… Like, sometimes it was great because I just wanted to feel like a kid and be treated like a kid and it was a relief. (18-year-old female)

Communicating with and engaging children

The relationship between professional and child is significantly important in any contact with children. Part of developing the relationship is dependent on remembering certain principles that facilitate rather than shut down communication (Thurgood, 1990). For example, children do not usually respond to a formal interview format and are likely to remain silent to direct questioning (Atwool, 2000). To communicate with children effectively it is important to establish rapport and, to do so, one must get to a child's level, physically and verbally (Thurgood, 1990). This means utilizing child development knowledge to engage with children appropriately (Jones, 1990). The communication must proceed at a child's pace with the sensitivity to allow the child to lead the interview at times (Bray and Pugh, 1997; Hughes, 2005; Jones, 1990; Webb, 1996).

> I think, I know it's hard, but you really need to find a balance because...sometimes I just longed to feel like a kid and be treated that way, but other times, I felt years beyond my age and I just wanted to be treated like an adult...I think just [through] observation, I think you can pick up the vibes, and just be more aware of where they're [children are] at at a particular time. (18-year-old female)

Refreshments and rituals

Offering children a snack and a drink are also important considerations in engaging and communicating with them, as is celebrating various events such as a child's birthday or therapeutic milestones. These are important factors that define childhood. Each child needs to be treated as an individual. This can be done by 'workers sharing a special joke with the child; remembering birthdays and important occasions; remembering a child's favourite food and so on' (Thurgood, 1990, p.58). Making these things an essential part of the research or intervention process lets children know that an effort is being made to enter their world because they are important (James, 1989).

> Maybe, sort of, have...food and everything, that kind of thing. Sort of makes you feel more relaxed. (11-year-old female)

> Chockies, yeh. That's good. It doesn't make it so, by the book, you know, like okay I'm here to talk...but it makes it more relaxed I think, because I felt safer and...cared for and all that kind of thing. (18-year-old female)

Involving the child's family

The most important part of a child's living context is the family (Geldard and Geldard, 1997). For this reason, any contact with a child must consider how the child's primary carers can become partners in interactions with children (James, 1989). This is what Leach refers to as 'parent-friendly professionals', who show a genuine respect for and acceptance of the parent's place in the child's life (1990, p.174). The extent of the parents' involvement in interventions with children must be carefully assessed, taking into account the parents' abilities and the child's needs (James, 1989).

> I've probably told Mum more things than I have to Dad, because, like, Mum's around more and, like, she's there when I need, because Dad, like, he's mostly at work and when he comes home, like, he's a good dad and that, er...but Mum's always around. (13-year-old male)

> Mum was very good and helped by not making me, not rushing me to get it out [the disclosure]...Mum's very, very understanding about it...but, I mean, I guess every kid thinks their mum's the best, well, not every kid, but a lot of kids. (11-year-old female)

Interviewing children who have been abused for research using a child-centred approach

'Research with children is far more complicated than simplifying procedures used with adults or adapting equipment "down to size"' (Koocher and Keith-Spiegel, 1994, p.76). Weithorn and Scherer (1994) draw attention to the need for researchers to be aware of the authority they wield, particularly in relation to research with children. The age difference between the researcher and the researched is a key issue (France, Bendelow and Williams, 2000). Children, like many other vulnerable groups in society, may be particularly susceptible to coercion, manipulation and persuasion, as well as expertise and institutionally sanctioned power. Researchers must therefore be fully cognizant of these issues and take measures to prevent their use. These issues become particularly significant when involving children who have been abused in research. The particular vulnerabilities and risks for children who have been abused are discussed in greater detail in the next chapter.

An approach that respects children and that is child-orientated is therefore imperative (Mauthner, 1997). Fine and Sandstrom confess that, in research, 'getting to know children is fun...having a role that downplays one's authority removes many of the hassles of parenting' (1988, p.76). Yet balancing research requirements with a role that is relaxed and fun, ethically sound and mindful of risks to children is a complex task. Christensen (2004), from her research experiences with children, states that one needs to reflect on the type of data likely to be produced if one is concerned only with the research process rather than the agendas and priorities of the respondents. Christensen raises a number of key themes that are extremely pertinent to child-centred research, including a 'dialogical research process' that she calls entering into children's 'cultures of communication' (1999a, cited in Christensen, 2004, p.166). This means that it is important to understand the particular context within which children are being involved and the language they use in such contexts. Christensen lists a number of factors pertinent to this issue, such as the use of language in each context, and conceptual meanings and actions that give a picture of the connections between children and adults. Failure to take these issues into account can run the risk of inaccurate data being collected. For example, in child abuse, it is important for researchers and counsellors to be aware of the language children may use to explain and talk about their experiences of abuse. In our research, several child-centred measures mentioned earlier became an integral part of our research process. These included those described below.

Belief system

We believe that it is important to involve those we interview in 'some level of partnership' (Mullender *et al.* 2002, p.12). Yet adult perceptions of, and attitudes to, children and childhood can either inhibit or promote this process. Our progressive specialization in working therapeutically with children who have been abused has promoted a strong belief in the need to involve and consult children on all issues. Our child-centred practice attempts to ensure that children are central to all interventions. We believe that interventions must be tailored according to children's individual developmental needs. Children must be empowered through these interventions, which provides the foundation for our child-centred practice.

The research environment

The research environment can play an important part during the research process, in reducing risks to children who have been abused. The setting should be appropriate to the child's age and size, and be comfortable and safe (Koocher and Keith-Spiegel, 1994). Mullender *et al.* (2002) suggest that consideration must be given to getting the context right, and choosing a place where children will feel comfortable and able to talk.

For ethical reasons, our research interviews could not be conducted at the centre where the children had received counselling. This was to prevent the child and family having concerns about any impact on the relationships with counsellors and the agency. Neither was the home of the child an acceptable option as we believe that it is important to keep the child's natural, living environment free from any further association with the abuse (see, for example, McGee, 2000).

Premises for the research interviews were sought at locations with a family focus. These offered privacy and could be set up in a child-friendly way. A research resource box that comprised children's furniture (a small table and chairs), drawing materials, games, flowers, some attractive pictures for the walls, snacks and drinks, was developed and set up for each interview. It also included all the research equipment.

Engaging children

Developing trust with children and young people in a research situation is difficult yet imperative if the research interview is to be successful (Grover, 2004; Morrow and Richards, 1996). This requires that researchers need to understand children's language use and their 'conceptual meanings and actions' (Christensen, 2004, p.170). Communicating with children in a simple, honest way that conveys respect for them and using language that is age, ability and context appropriate is highly effective in building trust and rapport: 'Children must trust the person to whom they are telling their story and the professional must always take seriously what the child is saying' (Bannister *et al.*, 1990, p.xii). The primary author's experience as a children's therapist, and knowledge of the language children used within the child abuse therapy context assisted considerably in engaging with the child for the research interview (see Mudaly and Goddard, 2001a). In addition, all participants were encouraged to 'play' with the research equipment (tape and video recorder). They monitored the equipment and participated in changing tapes and checking that images on the video were clear. This approach gave them some measure of control over the research process and promoted a sense of partnership in the process.

Techniques for eliciting information from children

Child-centred approaches include a range of different techniques that promote children's ability to give their views and opinions on various issues. Children need to have the freedom to communicate 'in their own way, using the medium with which they feel most comfortable' (Grover, 2004, p.90). Some techniques include getting children to write stories about an issue, or do drawings. They can also include activity books about the research topic, role plays, discussions, and individual, as well as group, interviews (Butler *et al.*, 2003; Leonard, 2005). Children can be given the option of choosing a technique they relate to, which promotes their participation and is empowering to them. In using the individual interview approach, one must be mindful that this may not be a child's preferred medium. Therefore combining this technique with other child-friendly features – for example, playing a game or allowing the child to do a drawing while the interview takes place – is an example of child-centred practice. In our research, the in-depth interview format was used (the next chapter explains the rationale for choosing this method). However, the interview generally took the form of a conversation between the child and the primary author. The child chose either to draw pictures or play games during the research interview.

Engaging the child's family

In research with children who have been abused, support by the primary protective parent is essential. This promotes the child's participation in the research. It also ensures the child attends the research interview and receives support after it. However, the child may or may not want a parent present, depending on their anxiety at being with a stranger or their desire to convey their ideas in private (Alderson, 1995). The need to engage the child's family was crucial to the success of this project. The parents were engaged in a variety of ways. These included approaching them through their child's counsellor who had been involved with the family, and through letters and information that appeared friendly and open. Many parents expressed approval of this approach and said that it promoted their interest in our research.

Conclusion

Involving children who have been abused in research can empower them. It can promote a change in the way society views and treats children by allowing children's voices to be heard. For effective research with children, all researchers who study children should 'possess competencies in research methodology, statistics, developmental psychology, family studies and child/adolescent mental health' (Koocher and Keith-Spiegel, 1994, p.48). This view recognizes the need to regard children as people in their own right, and to respond to their particular developmental needs within the research process. Some ways of conducting effective research with children who have been abused include being sensitive to the ethical issues in such research and ensuring that these are not minimized (see Chapter 3). Effective research also requires one to be particularly sensitive to the vulnerabilities and needs of children (see Chapter 9). Having a child-centred approach is a 'way to ensure effective outcomes for children' (Gilligan, 1994, p.120) and declares that children are valued and protected.

CHAPTER 4

The Ethics of Listening
to Children in Research

I didn't tell many people before I left home, but yeah, the few people that I did would say 'Get out, do something about it.' But I was only what?...15 or something, I wasn't an adult. You're not exactly equipped with the emotional or mental stuff to do that.

18-year-old female

Introduction

The previous chapters have outlined the importance of talking directly to children who have been abused about their experiences of abuse. Yet involving these children in child abuse research raises many ethical issues. There appears to be increased risk of additional trauma when they are involved in processes that are non-therapeutic such as research. In addition, asking them about their victimization experiences is extremely sensitive and can be experienced as invasive and intrusive. The 'ethical, legal, and methodological issues related to asking children about their maltreatment histories' place researchers in a minefield of ethical dilemmas (Runyan, 2000, p.676). These issues include 'how and what to inform children and parents before asking for study participation, how to respond to the disclosure of maltreatment to minimize risk and maximize benefit, and other potential risks to child participants, such as interview-engendered distress' (Amaya-Jackson *et al.*, 2000, p.726).

The lack of clear standards may cause study investigators significant apprehension. It may also explain the lack of discussion in research literature about how these issues are handled (Amaya-Jackson *et al.*, 2000). But child-centred researchers are beginning to talk about and explore processes that promote children's voices to be heard through research (see, for example,

Christensen, 2004). This chapter is a further contribution to current literature on these approaches. It presents a detailed discussion of the various ethical dilemmas that arose in our research and how these were addressed. The chapter also exposes some of the dilemmas that remained unresolved and that may require further exploration and discussion by other researchers.

A theoretical overview of ethics in research with children who have been abused

When human beings are involved in research, their rights, privacy and welfare must be protected. Major considerations in social research involving human participation include:

- balancing the possible benefits of the study with the potential for causing harm to the participants

- ensuring voluntary and informed consent

- ensuring anonymity and confidentiality of data, and

- consideration of the possibility of abuse by the researcher or exploitation by the research process.

(See, for example, Berglund, 1995; Glantz, 1996; Grinnell, 1993, 1997.)

The question, according to Mullender *et al.*, that arises when children are involved in research is 'Is researching children different from researching adults?' (2002, p.6). Mullender *et al.* go on to state that this would depend on how one views children. If they are seen as 'vulnerable and in need of protection…[this] would tend to place them in a passive and ultimately silenced position' (Mullender *et al.*, 2002, p.6). What appears to be important rather, is the need to respect difference so that methods are developed to address these differences (France *et al.*, 2000). These differences may be present for any group lacking in power or vulnerability. In this regard, when children are involved in research there is a greater need to be mindful of their unique qualities, and to carefully assess and minimize risks to them. The issues to consider are how they understand the research process because of their developmental competencies and experiences, their limited social power and their ambiguous legal status, which both protects and limits their rights (Thompson, 1992). Ethical issues in regard to children are concerned therefore with their ability to give informed consent, their varying competence according to age and cognitive ability, and their vulnerability to exploitation in research.

Taking these factors into account, research with children who have been abused becomes an even more complex matter. The impact of abuse-related trauma may result in diminished self-esteem and impaired perceptions of their personal competence, and they may respond to new adults by being either too aloof or too familiar (Thompson, 1992). They may therefore be at greater risk in procedures that challenge their self-esteem or require focused attention with a stranger. It is essential therefore to reflect carefully on the risks, especially the psychological harm that may result from anxiety and fear (Wender, 1994).

Ethical issues in research involving children who have been abused

Research that involves interviewing children who have been abused forces the researcher to face ethical questions that can be avoided in indirect research or research with adults, where the obligations of the researcher are not so clear-cut (Thomas and O'Kane, 1998). Some ethical questions that arise include the following.

- Will involvement in research on child abuse re-traumatise children who have been abused?

- How do we balance these children's particular vulnerabilities whilst meeting the research objectives?

- Can these children provide informed and voluntary consent?

- How much information about the study (i.e. about child abuse) should be provided for a child to decide about participation?

- How can anonymity and confidentiality be ensured for the child's protection and safety?

These questions are discussed further below, in the context of how they were addressed in our research.

Will involvement in research on child abuse re-traumatize children who have been abused?

The conflict between the risks and benefits of research with children who have been abused and their welfare and rights raises many ethical concerns that include the following.

- The emotional and psychological impact on children who have been abused of providing information about the abuse that could cause further trauma to the child and/or hinder the child's recovery.

- The limited benefits of the research for the child as this type of research may be classified as non-therapeutic having no direct or only minor benefit to the child (Koocher and Keith-Spiegel, 1994). Is it justifiable to involve a child who has been abused in such research procedures?

- What are the possible long-term consequences for children who have been abused of participating in such research?

These concerns have to be carefully balanced with the value, importance and rights of children who have been abused to be involved in research (Berliner and Conte, 1990; Butler et al., 2003; Runyan, 2000). In addition, children's vulnerability must also be considered. Vulnerability is an intrinsic part of children's development based on their developmental needs and dependence on adults to provide for their needs (see Chapter 10). This is increased by extrinsic social, cultural and environmental factors (which may include abuse). Intrinsic factors are inherent in the child and include cognitive, emotional, sensory deficiencies, physical defects and health issues (Cooke, 1994). Yet, if the perspective of the child is not sought, 'research, like practice, risks misperceiving the wishes, needs and interests of children' (Hill, 1997, p.172). Particular processes must therefore be introduced to address these concerns. In our research, careful thought was given to this complex issue and many measures were incorporated into the research procedures to minimize the above-mentioned risks to the children who participated.

- It was ensured that all children who were invited to participate in the research had had access to specific abuse-focused therapy (Briere, 2004). We believed that it was important for the children to have received therapy from a child-centred agency that specialized in abuse-related therapy. This meant that the therapy was provided in terms of each child's specific needs and they would therefore have had the opportunity of addressing the impact of their abusive experiences. Their sensitivity around the abuse would therefore probably be lessened (see, for example, Briere, 2004; James, 1989). Involvement in the research would also possibly be experienced as less intrusive. In addition, the established relationship with their counsellors would ensure their access to further counselling and support if needed following their involvement in the research.

At the conclusion of the research interview, none of the participants required follow-up therapy. Some participants who chose to talk about the abuse had become distressed during the process but it appeared that debriefing after the research interview had sufficiently addressed their distress. This may indicate that participation in the research had not contributed to further trauma, which we discuss in further detail later on. It may also point to the benefits and effectiveness of abuse-focused therapy as described by Briere (2004) as a precursor to involving these children in child abuse research.

- All children had decided on their own, with no apparent coercion or pressure from their parent, to participate in the study. The children's counsellors were able to check this out with the children. It was further confirmed by the primary author just prior to the research interview.

- There was no pressure for the children to verbalize details of the abuse in the research interview. Those who chose to do so, did so of their own free will.

- The child's main carer, the non-offending parent, was supportive of the research, felt comfortable with the research process and with his/her rights to question the process. The parent was assured of unbiased service if their child chose not to participate in the research.

- Child-centred counselling techniques were utilized as part of the research interview to engage the children, promote their ability to tell their story and for debriefing after the research interview (see Chapter 3). Attention was also given to whether the child wished to have their non-offending parent present at the interview. None of the children expressed a need to have a parent present. This may have been because, having had counselling, they were comfortable to be interviewed on their own.

- All the children were given the option of withdrawing from the research at any time, and of deleting, changing or adding to the information they had provided in the research interview. Follow-up appointments were specifically arranged for this purpose. None of the children chose to withdraw from the research, nor change the information they had provided. In fact all of them expressed delight at seeing themselves on video (see the next chapter, which discusses our reasons for video-taping the interviews). Many children verbalized how impressed they were with the information they had provided.

We believe that the children who participated in our research had not been re-traumatized by the research process. Trauma is described as 'an emotional shock that creates substantial, lasting damage to an individual's psychological development' (James, 1989, p.1). It may result from an incident that is sudden, unexpected and overwhelmingly intense (Terr, 1990). During the research interview, some children had experienced what Amaya-Jackson *et al.* (2000, p.726) refer to as 'interview-engendered distress'. However, it does not appear that they were further traumatized by involvement in the research. This may have been due to the many measures we had implemented to minimize this risk. However, we believe that there is a high possibility of interview-engendered trauma in child abuse research involving children who have been abused. We would therefore suggest that while it is possible to involve these children in child abuse research and not contribute to their further trauma, researchers must pay particular attention to addressing this issue as part of the research design.

The need to balance these children's particular vulnerabilities while meeting the research objectives

Balancing sensitivity to children's vulnerabilities and meeting the research objectives, – that is, getting the research completed – is a particularly difficult issue. All children by law have limited competence (Cooke, 1994). This is especially in regard to understanding and making decisions, but children with physical or mental disabilities or who have had traumatic experiences including abuse may be regarded as more vulnerable. This may result in an inadequate understanding of the risks and benefits of the research thereby having an impact on their ability to make an informed decision (Cooke, 1994). In addition, because of their age and developmental vulnerability, the dynamics and impact of traumatic experiences on children may not be easy to assess in relation to engaging these children in research (Koocher and Keith-Spiegel, 1994). A further issue is that children's susceptibilities to research risks become even more complex because of individual differences between children. The developmental stages of children therefore must be a consideration and their susceptibility to research risks and their reactions to research procedures taken into account for ethically sensitive research.

Koocher and Keith-Spiegel (1994) make a number of suggestions on how to reduce risks in research with children, taking into account their vulnerabilities. These include:

- an honest assessment of questions about the importance of the research

- thoroughly searching the literature to learn about risky procedures and their sequelae

- if risks are unknown, a small pilot sample should be run to check out risk elements

- all experimental equipment should be assessed for safety from the 'child's eye' (p.57)

- where some risk is expected, such as any discomfort, extended duration of the data collection or where very young children are involved, then the presence of a parent or carer must be viewed as an ethical necessity.

Other measures include having a developmental orientation in relation to the age and developmental level of potential child subjects, graded rather than threshold judgements of risk, focusing on risk rather than benefit, and giving consideration to the special characteristics of the research population (Stanley and Sieber, 1992). Attention is drawn to the need for the researcher to be knowledgeable about children's particular vulnerabilities and capacities, always attending to the social and psychological child as well as the biological child. Some authors call for the use of developmental researchers on ethical review boards or as invited consultants in the research review process (Thompson, 1992). Others state that when children and adolescents are involved, ethical vigilance becomes more necessary (see, for example, Macklin, 1992). Respecting children's competencies should become a methodological technique utilizing an approach that gives children control over the research process and allowing them to participate on their own terms (Macklin, 1992; Morrow and Richards, 1996).

Just being aware of these issues in the research process is not enough. Strategies and procedures need to be incorporated throughout the research process to ensure that children's vulnerabilities are neither compromised nor become subordinate to the research objectives. Berg (1998, p.52) states that this places the researcher in an 'ethical bind'. On the one hand researchers want to advance knowledge and understanding in a rigorous manner, on the other they need to be careful not to violate the rights of participants nor expose them to potential long-term harm. From the outset of our research, many months were spent researching and reading current literature on research with children who have been abused with particular attention to the child protection field. An analysis of several cases at a children's therapy centre was undertaken. Presentations and discussions at postgraduate seminars at Monash University explored the various ethical dilemmas. Through these efforts it became increasingly evident that the research would be important as it would provide children who have been abused with the opportunity to have their voices about their experiences of abuse heard.

Being a children's therapist with particular experience in treating child victims of abuse made the primary author especially aware of the children's vulnerabilities. Of significance was our stipulation that all the children had to have had therapeutic interventions that had addressed their abusive experiences. This reduced their fear and sensitivity to their experiences (see earlier discussion). We paid particular attention to choosing a research methodology so as to minimize risks to potential participants. The qualitative methodology 'assumes that minors are knowledgeable about their worlds, that these worlds are special and noteworthy, and that we as adults can benefit by viewing the world through their hearts and minds' (Fine and Sandstrom, 1988, p.12). This methodology promoted children's involvement in the research process as partners and allowed them to tell their stories in their own voices. Further details about the methodology are discussed in the next chapter.

Another checkpoint to ensure that these matters had been considered was addressed by the Monash University Standing Committee on ethics in research with human subjects. As part of our application for ethics approval to conduct the research, we were required to make a written and verbal presentation to the Committee. At this meeting, we had to identify these risk factors and explain how they would be managed and minimized in the research process.

In conclusion, we believe that the measures that were implemented to minimize re-traumatizing these children through involvement in the research, also ensured that their vulnerabilities (related to childhood, and to the abuse) were carefully addressed.

Consent issues

Consent issues in child abuse research with children who have been abused raise a plethora of critical ethical dilemmas. Many questions arise, such as:

- Can these children give informed and voluntary consent?
- How much information about the research topic should be provided for children to consent to participation?
- Would providing detailed information on child abuse be harmful?
- When parents consent, is it in a child's best interests?

All these questions were carefully considered and we report on them here.

CHILDREN'S INFORMED AND VOLUNTARY CONSENT

There are many tensions that exist in obtaining informed consent from children for their participation in any research (Edwards and Alldred, 1999). This includes the child's age and competence and the legal status of children. Because of these issues, children can only *assent* to their participation in research; parents have the legal responsibility and power to *consent* to children's participation (Tymchuk, 1992). However, in child abuse research with children who have been abused, the issue of children's assent and parents' consent needs further exploration.

THE CHILD'S ASSENT

Several issues that must be considered include:

- the child's competence or ability to assent
- providing information about the study so that a child can decide about participation
- whether children's assent can be voluntary.

Competency or capacity, intelligence or maturity refer to skills, abilities, knowledge and experience to make a decision about one's participation with a full understanding of one's rights and the risks involved from such participation (Weithorn and Scherer, 1994). This is regarded as *informed consent* (Glantz, 1996). Legally it is acknowledged that children are not able to enter into such agreements. Therefore parents or guardians must provide such permission. When children agree to participate, this is referred to as assent. For ethically sound research with children, both parents and children should be involved in the assent procedures (Grinnell, 1993, 1997; Kinard, 1985; Tymchuk, 1992). It is in children's interests as well as the interests of their parents and the researcher to maximize children's involvement in decisions about their participation in research. Alderson (1995) offers a checklist to promote children's consent in an informed and freely chosen process. She suggests that they must be given time to think about participation, as well as reassurances that refusal would not compromise them in any way. Consideration must also be given to whether they wish a parent to be present or not, in addition to choosing a research context that would promote and not inhibit their participation. For example, we chose venues for the research interview that were child-centred (see Chapter 3).

An important factor for children to agree to participate in research is the need to provide them with adequate information about the study. They can then make an informed decision about participation. Potential participants must be provided 'with clear and unambiguous information about the purpose and nature of the particular research study' (Edwards and Alldred, 1999, p.266). However, harm may result from information that appears to label a child who has been abused, or is deceitful, or which holds back important information (Kinard, 1985). Providing detailed information about the full nature of research on abuse can also alarm children who have been abused. On the other hand, too little information may not give them an accurate picture of the research in order for them to decide to participate. Other related issues, such as avoiding adult-framed questions and answers, also create ethical problems for the researcher (Morrow and Richards, 1996). Children's ages and cognitive abilities must be a major consideration in this regard. Researchers in the field of childhood point out that chronological age and competence are not the same and that even young children who are provided with age-appropriate information can make informed decisions (Berglund, 1995; Edwards and Alldred, 1999; Grinnell, 1993, 1997). Obtaining a balance of providing enough information in a manner that is developmentally appropriate and that encourages children's participation in child abuse research is a difficult and sensitive issue.

In our research we gave careful thought to how much information about the research would be adequate and how the information would be conveyed to the participants. A child-centred approach was chosen to present the information in a manner comprehensible and accessible to children's level of development. The information was prepared in a two-page, simple question-and-answer format, which included questions such as: What is this study about? What will be discussed? Will the names of participants and the information be confidential? What support will be available after the interview? The information was presented in different colours to make the package child-friendly and appealing. An interesting idea described by Butler *et al.* (2003) is the use of a newsletter format. This allows for photographs and information about the researchers to be included (such as their expertise to carry out sensitive research). It is also less formal than university letterheads. This is certainly a suggestion worth considering in research with children.

To promote the joint involvement of the child and parent in our study, they were first informed briefly about the research by the child's counsellor with whom they had developed a trusting and secure relationship. The subsequent explanatory letter with information about the study, an invitation to participate in the research, and their rights not to participate was prepared by the primary author but sent out by the child's counsellor. The letter was addressed both to the child and the parent. They were reassured that neither their counselling nor their relationship with the agency would be affected in any way by their decision. A short note to the child, handwritten by the counsellor, was added, explaining the counsellor's reason for selecting the child. It was envisaged that this personal note to the child from his/her counsellor would demonstrate the counsellor's approval of the research, alleviate any anxiety the child might have about the research and maximize the child's involvement in deciding about participating in the research. The letter also explained that the researcher had no identifying information about the child or the family during this consent phase. This approach of recruiting potential research participants, where they have to make an active decision to participate by contacting the researcher, protects their anonymity (McGee, 2000). The opportunity to clarify information prior to consenting, whereby the child and parent could speak further to their counsellor or the researcher, was also offered.

The third question that needs to be considered and responded to on the issue of consent is whether children's assent can be voluntary. The concept of voluntariness implies 'substantial absence of control by others' (Weithorn and Scherer, 1994, p.142). These authors suggest that coercion, manipulation and persuasion are potentially controlling factors and that children are more susceptible to such influences. Potential participants must be given maximum freedom to agree or refuse to participate and must believe that they have this choice. This means that considering the child's emotional and social context is essential when deciding on the criteria for the research sample. This requires being aware that the competency of participants who are ill, tired, confused or experiencing other disruptions may be impaired. It is important therefore that 'the demands of the environment are minimised and the capacities of the individual to respond to choice are optimal' (Weithorn and Scherer, 1994, p.143).

Being particularly conscious of the impact of abuse and of children's dependence on their adult carers, our criteria for children's participation were carefully decided on and as stated earlier in this chapter. That is, that children had had abuse-focused therapy and that a non-offending parent supported the child's participation. Children's counsellors were also reminded that potential research participants had to be safe from any known abuse and that there were no current concerns about the child's protection and care. In addition, the research interviews were not conducted in the child's home in order to keep the living situation free from abuse-related issues. It was hoped that these precautions would provide the foundation for and promote the voluntary consent of both children and their parents to participate in the research. However, despite these considerations, there may have been some influence and/or control in the following ways.

1.   The relationship that develops between the child and his/her counsellor. The counsellor's support for the research could have been experienced as subtly coercive in that the child may not have felt free to refuse to participate out of anxiety at upsetting his/her counsellor.

2.   The parents could have coerced or persuaded the children to participate in order to maintain a positive and co-operative relationship with the agency.

To minimize these influences, the child's decision to participate was clarified with each child just prior to the research interview, when they were given the opportunity to withdraw from the study. A follow-up appointment was also offered and arranged, when each child was given a further chance to change or delete information they had provided in the research interview. McGee (2000) discusses a technique to help children to be assertive in saying no to questions they do not feel comfortable about answering. In her research on domestic violence, just prior to the research interview, she got children to practise saying no in a fun manner. This is an excellent idea.

PARENTAL CONSENT

Parental consent for children to participate in research is another subject that is problematic in this type of research. As children are legally not allowed to consent to their participation in research, it is generally considered that a parent or guardian may be the appropriate person to consent for the child. They are presumed to act in the child's best interests (Kinard, 1985). This can become complicated if parents have their own interests. With children who have been abused this may become even more complex since parents' interests may conflict with those of the child. This may be more so if a child is being exposed to or experiencing some form of abuse.

One procedure used in our study to prevent conflict between parent and child was to obtain the parent's support for the research. When selecting potential participants, counsellors were asked to consider those families where parents were assessed as protective and supportive of their children. Counsellors then consulted the parent about the research and elicited their interest. To promote the child's participation in the consent phase, a request for the research to be explained to the child was made in the introductory letter that was addressed to the child and parent. Separate spaces were provided on the consent form for the child and parent to sign their consent. It was interesting to note that there were various responses from parents and children. In some instances parents made the decision, without consulting their children, for the children not to participate in the research. They felt that it would be traumatic for their children. In other cases, children refused to participate even though their parents were interested in the research. It was reassuring to note that these parents did not pressure their children into participation despite their own support for the research.

Some researchers explore the notion of actively recruiting children and bypassing parental gatekeepers (see Thomas and O'Kane, 1998). This approach can be empowering to children and maximizes their participation. However, we believe that this would be difficult in any research on child abuse that involves children who have been abused. There are a number of essential considerations in this regard. Support during and after the research interview, follow-up counselling if the need arose, transporting to and from the research interview are parental responsibilities. The involvement of parents or a child's carer in interventions with children who have been abused is not only essential but crucial as it is imperative that the child's safety and need for protection remains the primary consideration. Ultimately, the responsibility for the abuse and children's recovery must be with the non-offending parents (Mannarino and Cohen, 1990). We believe that non-offending parents have to be seen as partners in research that involves children who have been abused. We also believe that these are some of the issues that make research with children who have been abused different and that therefore call for special considerations and methods to be used.

How can anonymity and confidentiality be ensured for the child's protection and safety?

Protection of privacy is a basic right of all research participants (Grinnell, 1993; Koocher and Keith-Spiegel, 1994; Melton, 1992) but this becomes a problem when the research is about child abuse and when it involves children who have been abused. The conflict arises from assuring confidentiality to children about the information they provide in the research interview and giving feedback about their responses to a parent or others. A further concern is about how disclosures of current abuse by children during the research interview should be responded to. Two recent trends that are emerging question whether parents have an absolute right to know everything about their child and, second, the increasing recognition of children's rights to privacy (Koocher and Keith-Spiegel, 1994). Leach (1990, p.180) explains this complexity:

> The benevolent authoritarianism that dominates our attitudes to children as objects of concern does not only frustrate professionals' attempts to work for individual children within their families, it often directly infringes children's human rights in ways that have long been outlawed for adults.

Another pertinent issue in research is that of anonymity. The difference between confidentiality and anonymity, according to Berg (1998), is that in qualitative research, because subjects are known to the researcher, anonymity is essentially non-existent. For this reason a high degree of confidentiality needs to be provided to research participants. Yet this may become difficult when the need to share information with parents or others is seen as being of significant benefit to the child. The child, though, may not want information about his or her responses or performance in the research to be shared with others. An added difficulty is that when parents consent to their child's participation they may request or expect detailed feedback, especially if the research topic is on a subject of concern or interest to them (Koocher and Keith-Spiegel, 1994).

In our research, this was a difficult issue to resolve, both in principle and in practice. Assuring children of their right to decide what information could be shared with their parents and others conflicts with a professional's duty to notify authorities if concerns about a child's safety arise. In regard to providing feedback to people other than the parent, the guiding principle is that this should be done with consent from the parent and the 'free and informed permission' of the child prior to the research interview (Koocher and Keith-Spiegel, 1994, p.66). However, a researcher must also be aware of the limitations on children's freedom to do this because of their dependence on parents and because of parental role power. Koocher and Keith-Spiegel (1994) discuss some options for overcoming this dilemma, such as setting ground rules for information sharing with both parents and children at the outset. This could assist children in deciding what and how much information they wish to divulge in the research interview.

In our study, the parent and child were informed just prior to the research interview that the child and primary author would give brief feedback to the parent after the interview. The parent and child were also reminded at this time about sharing information with others, in particular the primary author's responsibilities related to concerns about a child's safety. Children were given several options on how feedback to parents and therapists could occur. Just prior to completion of the research interview, the primary author worked out with the child what information would be given to the parent. The child and primary author agreed to do this together. Feedback to the child's therapist was also decided with the child, what the content of the feedback would be, and how this would be conveyed. In most cases, there was no need for feedback to the therapists. Where it was required (in one case), the child felt comfortable for the primary author to do this in his absence.

Responding to disclosures of current or ongoing abuse during the research interview, as well as making a report of the disclosures to authorities, creates a major ethical dilemma. It conflicts with any assurance of confidentiality to the child and parent (Kinard, 1985; Runyan, 2000). Researchers appear to fall into one of two categories. Some strongly believe that 'certificates of confidentiality should never be used to supersede state laws on reporting', and others believe that 'ethically sound research could include cases of child maltreatment detected but unrecorded by the researcher and unreported to authorities' (Runyan, 2000, p.677). However, whether mandated or not, Kinard (1985) believes that professionals need to place the safety of a child above legal obligations. They should be morally and ethically bound to report. Withholding information from those who could alleviate the problem is regarded by Koocher and Keith-Spiegel (1994) as inappropriate. They suggest this could be handled effectively at the consent phase. As there are no clear-cut guidelines about what is legally and ethically expected of research investigators (Amaya-Jackson *et al.*, 2000), researchers tend to provide explanations for their particular approach.

In our research, we strongly supported the proponents of the first point of view, believing that any risk of harm to a child during the research process 'should be recognised and that steps should be taken to offer protection' (Runyan, 2000, p.677). An assurance of confidentiality was therefore qualified by the primary author's responsibility to report any disclosures pertaining to a child's safety. This was explained in the introductory letter and information pamphlet. The principle was further mentioned to the child and parent just prior to the research interview and again repeated to the child during the interview. It is likely that some parents (and children) chose not to participate in the research because of this principle.

Thomas and O'Kane (1998) believe that not assuring full confidentiality would have an impact on a child's trust in the researcher. They believe that children and young people should be empowered in the research process by allowing them the autonomy to decide what they wanted to say and to whom they wanted to say it. Their view about disclosures of abuse was that if the child is ready to have this information passed on, their role as researchers would be to help the child tell someone in authority rather than making the report themselves. The idea of empowering children by allowing them to decide what they wished to say in the research interview and trusting the researcher is a positive one. However, the principle of assuring full confidentiality is problematic. It is our view that such an approach can be confusing to children. Being consistent and clear about one's moral and ethical responsibilities are essential qualities that children come to accept as part of adult roles and responsibilities. Having to break the commitment to confidentiality in an 'exceptional' situation (Thomas and O'Kane, 1998, p.340) could be viewed by the child as having been lied to and deceived (Kinard, 1985). It could impair the child's relationship, not only with the researcher, but with adults in general. While we took a clear stance on this issue, we recognize that this approach has implications for any child abuse research involving children who have been abused.

Limitations to addressing ethical dilemmas in child abuse research with children who have been abused

Despite being particularly aware of the ethical issues and vulnerabilities of these children and also developing strategies to minimize research risks, there were many limitations to the free and informed participation of the children. The following questions were not fully resolved at the conclusion of our study.

- Is it ethically acceptable in research with children who have been abused for them to experience emotional pain associated with talking about their abusive experiences?

- Can children be true partners in research when they are not legally allowed to consent to their own participation?

- Can full confidentiality in research with children who have experienced abuse be assured?

While many strategies can be employed to reduce or minimize the pain associated with remembering abusive experiences there are no guidelines to assist researchers on how to protect children who have been abused from the impact of the research, the research interview or procedures that cause distress (Runyan, 2000). In our research, while there was no pressure for participants to talk about the abuse, many children chose to do so. They admitted that it had been difficult. At the same time, they conveyed that they had felt better after they had spoken about the abuse. Although all the participants were fully debriefed after the research interview, and most did not require follow-up counselling as a result of their participation in the research, we felt uncomfortable that they had experienced emotional pain during the interview. The lack of suggestions in the literature on how to minimize and respond to interview-engendered distress to child participants in child abuse research has prompted Runyan to argue for further research on this issue. He states that little 'is known about the impact of research procedures and benefit and harm to child participants' (Runyan, 2000, p.680).

   The second issue is the importance of encouraging children and young people to be partners in any research involving them (Weithorn and Scherer, 1994). In child abuse research with children who have been abused, the concerns about competency and ability to consent presents a dilemma for childhood researchers who want to 'treat children as active subjects of research rather than passive objects, to hear their voices, and to respect and empower them' (Edwards and Alldred, 1999, p.266). As we have seen, children can only 'assent' to their participation in research and, inevitably, the decision by their parents overrides whatever the child's view may be (Thomas and O'Kane, 1998). The child's free and informed assent is also limited by a variety of factors such as dependence on their parents, and the coercion, manipulation and persuasion that children, in particular children who have been abused, may be more susceptible to (Berglund, 1995; Weithorn and Scherer, 1994). In addition, not being able to assure full confidentiality to a child in relation to their protection or safety, draws attention to the unequal status between child and researcher. All these factors have an impact on whether children can be regarded as true partners in research.

Guaranteeing full confidentiality to children who have been abused and who are involved in research on child abuse is another complicated matter, as discussed in detail earlier in this chapter. The principle adopted by Thomas and O'Kane (1998) to assure full confidentiality, and to break this in exceptional situations or help the child make a report to the authorities if he/she discloses abuse, is a contentious one. Yet, providing only conditional confidentiality seems to emphasize the child's lack of equal status to the researcher. This could have an impact on the trust between the researcher and the child (Thomas and O'Kane, 1998). In our research, our belief in the need to make notifications to the relevant authorities if there were disclosures of abuse conflicted with our equally strong belief in empowering and promoting children's rights to be heard and their right to privacy. This is a discomfort that we have had to contend with as part of the many conflicts and contradictions inherent in this type of research.

In the absence of answers to these ethical concerns, King and Churchill (2000) believe that a full moral analysis by the researcher is necessary. An analysis that explains and justifies a researcher's choices and demonstrates the thoughtful, deliberative process followed, and that is available for examination, are 'significant features of responsible research policy and practice' (King and Churchill, 2000, p.723). The lack of ethical guidelines means that these are some of the hurdles and frustrations researchers must navigate in order to advance knowledge on children (Koocher and Keith-Spiegel, 1994). Amaya-Jackson *et al.* state that 'the lack of a clear set of standards for ethical research in the area of child maltreatment may cause study investigators significant apprehension and may explain the lack of discussion in research literature about how these issues are handled' (2000, p.727).

It is suggested that in the absence of ethical guidelines to conduct research with children who have been abused, there should be ethical principles to guide researchers.

Ethical principles

While the limitations of using principles to guide research with children are acknowledged, principles can provide clarity and understanding of ethical tools that researchers can use to help them grapple with issues that arise in their studies (King and Churchill, 2000; Thompson, 1992). The major principles of research ethics include that the research results must be significant and provide answers to questions important to the welfare of children. They must also hold substantial promise of benefit to children. They must be scientifically sound in that the study must be 'well designed and meticulously carried out by "qualified researchers" who are especially careful and reflective about methodological issues' (King and Churchill, 2000, p.713). Other principles include a respect for autonomy (research participants' freedom to choose and act without constraints imposed by others); as well as the 'beneficence' and 'nonmaleficence' factors, which refer to benefit and prevention of harm for the participant (King and Churchill, 2000, p.714; Thompson, 1992). These must be carefully considered and declared. The research should demonstrate that the substantial benefits would outweigh any harms for the research participants themselves. The principle of justice in research with abused children applies to disclosing the full risks of harm to participants. It also emphasizes researchers' duties in regard to confidentiality, and that consideration is given to the specific vulnerabilities of the research participants. Littlechild (2000) suggests that ethical principles also need to be applied in daily interventions and practice with children who have been abused. He suggests that it is imperative to be clear with children about the limited nature of confidentiality. One must explain the possibility of giving evidence in court, provide full information about the system, meetings and hearings, and how children can participate in these, and give practical details about how and by whom they will be supported throughout the process (Littlechild, 2000).

Ethical standards must also be applied throughout a research project, not only in the design stage but also at the dissemination stage. In addition, for ethical research it is a requirement that researchers have 'technical competence' using the highest standards of social science investigation procedures (Peled and Leichtentritt, 2002, p.150). From an analysis of several randomly-selected published social work research studies on attention to ethical issues Peled and Leichtentritt (pp.160–1) report that 'most overlook ethical issues most of the time'. They conclude that 'most qualitative social work researchers pay little or no attention to ethical issues in their studies' (pp.160–1). They further state that researchers who are highly committed to ethical standards would not overlook these principles while reporting their results.

Our research has weathered the ethical dilemmas that are inherent in child abuse studies that directly ask children about abuse as best it could in order to carry out and complete the research. It has required much contemplation, research, sensitivity and discussion. This chapter has openly declared and reported on the dilemmas, strategies employed and the many unresolved ethical issues. We acknowledge that there may be strategies or issues that we have overlooked. At the time of conducting our research, we considered as many issues that we could identify and addressed them to the best of our ability.

CHAPTER 5

A Chance to be Heard
Involving Children who have been Abused in Research

Yeah…I'd love to help in research cos research will be good, research usually, um, ends up as a worthwhile cause and that's why I'm telling, because it is really researching.

11-year-old female

Introduction

This book is about child abuse by children who have been abused. The previous chapters have drawn attention to two important issues:

1. The rights of children who have been abused to have their voices heard.

2. The importance of being particularly sensitive to their vulnerabilities and needs when involving them in research processes.

For this reason the choice of a research methodology that addressed these issues and was empowering of the research participants had to be carefully considered. Qualitative research appeared to be an appropriate methodology. It: 'assumes that minors are knowledgeable about their worlds, that these worlds are special and noteworthy, and that we as adults can benefit by viewing the world through their hearts and minds' (Fine and Sandstrom, 1998, p.12)

This book is based on a study that attempted to understand abuse through the descriptions of abuse by children who had been abused. Much of this book presents the experiences of abuse in the words of the children themselves.

The rationale for choosing a qualitative methodology

The primary goal of this research was to provide the opportunity for the voices of children who had experienced abuse to be heard. More specifically, it aimed to present children's voices on their experiences of abuse; how they understood the abuse and its impact on their lives; their feelings about the abuser and non-offending parent(s); and their perceptions of the help offered them by professionals mandated to ensure their protection and recovery. The traditional, positivist social science research methods from which much child abuse information was historically derived does not allow for the subjective realm of victims of abuse to be explored. The value and importance of the qualitative method is now gaining more attention and becoming more popular in studies involving human beings (Strauss and Corbin, 1998). This methodology 'attempts to capture people's meanings, definitions and descriptions of events' (Minichiello *et al.*, 1995, p.9). According to Denzin and Lincoln, qualitative research is 'a family of terms, concepts, and assumptions' (2000, p.2). It draws upon a range of approaches and methods that attempt to allow subjects to communicate their own experiences. These include 'techniques of ethnomethodology, phenomenology, hermeneutics, feminism, rhizomatics, deconstructionism, ethnography, interviews, psychoanalysis, cultural studies, survey research, and participant observation, among others' (p.6).

For researchers who use this methodology, there is a commitment to 'the naturalistic perspective and to the interpretive understanding of human experience' (Denzin and Lincoln, 2000, p.7). This method allows people to tell their own stories in their own voices, promotes new realities to be discovered by interactive dialogue between researchers and participants, and prevents the need to find simple answers to complex life issues (Berg, 1998). It allows for the multiple realities of the many persons whose voices have been silenced to be reflected. It also examines how people learn about and make sense of themselves and others (Berg, 1998; Hudson and Nurius, 1994). It is therefore rich in description and colourful in detail (Grover, 2004; Neuman, 1997).

In choosing a qualitative research method, it is important that the research question should dictate the method rather than a researcher's orientation towards a specific method (Strauss and Corbin, 1998). This approach prevents the risk of children being analysed according to 'adult theoretical categories that serve adult agendas' (Grover, 2004, p.83). It has the added advantage of building social work knowledge by providing an important opportunity to inform practice from the child's perspective.

Butler *et al.* (2003) draw attention to some of the dilemmas in utilizing this methodology. These include 'how to present findings that are "true" to the underlying phenomena that are being studied' (p.14); that data collection and analysis are not completely value free, objective and neutral; and that we have to decide on the plausibility of children's accounts – that is, that they are meaningful, make sense and are relevant to the issue under study. This last point becomes less of a problem when the children's words are the primary data. We echo these authors when they say 'In the final analysis (as it were), it will be for the reader to decide how "honest" our analysis and presentation of data have been' (p.15).

Hearing participants' voices in research

In the past, the only voice in research was the 'voice from nowhere', abstract representations of research participants in the texts (Lincoln and Guba, 2000, p.183). Today, 'voice' means letting participants speak for themselves, which prevents the researcher writing in the 'distanced and abstracted voice of the disembodied "I"' (p.183). Other factors that are important in this methodology include reflexivity, or the process of reflecting critically on the self as the researcher, both as an inquirer and as a respondent (Flick, 1998). Our views and reflections are based on the research process, data and issues raised by the children.

The research design

In accordance with the primary aim of this research to give children who had been abused a voice, the research design was governed by a set of principles and ethics that guided the research as it progressed (Denzin and Lincoln, 2000). Honesty, openness of intent, respect for the participants, issues of privacy, anonymity, confidentiality and voluntary participation were carefully appraised at the design stage (Berg, 1998). Of particular importance is the need for and importance of the study.

The need for the study arose from the primary author's professional involvement with children who had been abused. From an initial literature review, it became evident that there was limited research undertaken directly with children who had been abused. A major limitation to involving victimized children in research was around the ethical issues that are significant to this type of research and that were explored in detail in the previous chapter.

In order to determine the need for and value of this research, an examination of several cases of children who had experienced neglect, physical, emotional and sexual abuse, and domestic violence, and who had received therapy for the abuse was undertaken. From this case analysis, and after many consultations with interested and concerned peers, and presentations at postgraduate seminars, the decision to proceed with the research was established.

Securing a sample

The ideal site for conducting a research programme is one where the researcher is able to gain easy access; where a high probability of the subject material of interest to the researcher is present; one that facilitates the researcher to build a trusting relationship with the participants in the study; and where the quality of the data and credibility of the study will be assured (Marshall and Rossman, 1995). The therapy centre from where the sample of research participants was drawn was chosen because of the authors' professional association with the centre over many years. Both authors had intimate knowledge of and confidence in the philosophy and therapeutic approaches practised by this centre. We felt assured that a suitable sample of research participants could be recruited (Australian Childhood Foundation, 2001, 2003; Centre for Children, 1999). It was also felt that this centre would welcome feedback from its clients on its therapeutic services and would take the necessary steps to implement any changes that may be required to improve its services. In addition, the organization was renowned in the state for advocating on behalf of children who had experienced abuse. We felt assured that the research would gain credibility and promote children's voices through association with this centre.

Recruiting the sample

Children who were invited to participate in the study were chosen using the purposive or concrete sampling method as the sample was limited in advance by specified criteria (Padgett, 1998). These criteria were determined by the focus of the study (children who had been assessed as victims of abuse by child protection services and/or the police), the limitations set by the Monash University Standing Committee on Ethics in Research on Humans (children over the age of seven years who had *not* been counselled by the primary author), and the criteria set by us to minimize the effects of re-traumatizing the participants through the research process (see previous chapter). This included the need for therapeutic intervention as a prerequisite to research participation (Cooke, 1994; Kinard, 1985; Koocher and Keith-Spiegel, 1994).

Recruitment of the sample used the 'opt-in' procedure, which meant that participants had to make an active decision to be involved in the study. In contrast, the 'opt-out' procedure allows researchers access to identifying details of potential participants who must then actively refuse to be involved in the study (Butler *et al.*, 2003; McGee, 2000). The opt-in procedure protects the identities of potential participants until they opt to participate in the project. This stance promotes an ethical approach when children who have been abused are invited to participate in research. Details of this process were described in the previous chapter. In in-depth, interpretive research, the size of the sample is irrelevant as the focus of the research is on capturing detailed descriptions in their own words and terms about the life-worlds of children who have been abused (Berg, 1998).

Of the 29 invitations that were sent out to prospective participants, nine children and their carers consented to participate in the study. Of these, five were male and four female. The ages ranged from nine to eighteen years. Cultural issues were not significant in selecting the sample as the research was open to all children who met the criteria. All the children who participated in the study were Australian born and some were of European descent. Many of the children in the sample had experienced multiple forms of abuse. This verified what many researchers have found, that victims of abuse are rarely subject to only one form of abuse (Browne, Davies and Stratton, 1988; Goddard, 1996; McGee, 2000; Stanley and Goddard, 2002; Tomison, 2000). Sexual abuse was the most common form of abuse, with seven out of the nine children having been sexually abused. All five males in the sample in comparison to two females had experienced physical abuse and family violence, a correlation identified by Goddard and Hiller (1993a). In addition, some of these children who had experienced violence and physical abuse were also victims of sexual abuse. This fact was again borne out in the study by Goddard and Hiller, who state that 'domestic violence is almost as common in cases of sexual abuse as it is in cases of physical abuse' (1993a, p.67).

Data collection and analysing procedures

Data collection in qualitative research may be one of several methods: participation in the setting, direct observation, in-depth interviewing and document review (Marshall and Rossman, 1995; Padgett, 1998). The method chosen in this research was the in-depth interview using a child-centred approach (see Chapter 3). Using a child-centred approach is particularly significant as children may not respond to direct questioning (Atwool, 2000). The in-depth interview is a common method in qualitative research and is rather more like a conversation than a formal interview that has predetermined responses (Marshall and Rossman, 1995). It takes the form of a conversation between researcher and research participant with the focus on the participant's perception of self, life and experience expressed in his or her own words (Minichiello *et al.*, 1995).

In-depth interviewing is particularly useful in researching certain experiences or events such as child abuse. It allows a researcher to gain insight into activities and events that cannot be observed directly (Minichiello *et al.*, 1995). There are several types of in-depth interview such as the life history approach, or accessing groups of people to obtain a broad view of situations, people or settings. The clinical interview approach includes the counselling interview (Minichiello *et al.*, 1995). This approach best suited our research as its population was children who had experienced abuse. A major tenet of this method is the emphasis 'on allowing the client time to unfold his or her own story in his or her own way' (p.134).

We were interested in children's perceptions of abuse and related issues, which makes the unstructured interview process ideal as it promotes the uncovering of the participant's meanings and perspective (Kellehear, 1993; Marshall and Rossman, 1995). An important consideration in this type of approach is how to begin the research interview. Minichiello *et al.* (1995) suggest that there are two ways of beginning an unstructured research interview. The first is where the researcher provides little information about the research to avoid bias. The second approach is one where the researcher believes that collaborative research requires the participant to be armed with knowledge about the nature of the research, how the research will be conducted, and about confidentiality and anonymity issues, among others. It allows for researcher and researched to be involved in a process of negotiation and renegotiation on how the interview should and will proceed (see, for example, Pease and Goddard, 1996). In our research, we felt it was essential for the children to have a clear idea about important aspects of the research process to promote their informed participation. This included the nature of the research, the equipment that was to be used (audio- and video-tapes), conditional confidentiality (and the researcher's duty to report to child protection authorities if there were concerns about a child's current protection), as well as feedback to the parent after the research interview. We chose to inform potential participants about these issues through an information package that was sent out to them. They were also informed at the introductory phase of the interview.

The interview itself took the form of a conversation that allowed the child to decide which topic and issue he or she wished to talk about and how much information he or she wished to reveal. This approach provides gentle guidance and directs the flow of the interview at certain times (Padgett, 1998). It was interesting to note how structured and intent most children were as many chose to make a list of the topics that were to be discussed. Some verbalized this while others made a list and stuck it on the wall for easy reference. They kept a check on how they were progressing and which topics they wished to address or not talk about. Some children would summarize the topics covered and ask the primary author which ones still needed to be talked about. The quotes and extracts in this book have been taken directly from the research interviews where children chose to speak on specific topics, therefore they do not represent the experiences of all the children who participated in the research. At the end of the interview, children were given the option of deleting or adding further information or, if they preferred, a second interview. They were also given the option of viewing their video-taped interviews (and most of them did). They were then again given the choice to add to or delete the information they had provided. All the children who viewed their video-taped interviews were pleased to see themselves on video. The oldest participant, an 18-year-old young woman, contacted the researcher after the research interview and requested to have a second interview. Having thought about the various issues discussed, she had decided she wanted a further say on some topics. She chose not to delete any information from her first interview but had listed several other things she wanted to talk about. This included her experience of the child protection department and therapeutic services (see Chapter 8).

Butler et al. (2003) describe in detail the attention they gave to developing child-centred interviewing techniques. They developed a child-friendly activity book that comprised sections for an introduction to the research process, building rapport and collection of data. They used coloured pages, and children could draw and colour in certain sections. Butler et al. also included debriefing and fun activities to promote children's interest and attention. This is an impressive example of child-centred research.

Recording the data: the audio-visual record

The most commonly used methods of recording research interviews are through tape-recordings and note-taking (Minichiello *et al.*, 1995). Video-recording is now becoming more popular for recording of non-verbal data. It is an important, non-literate source of information for less literate and less verbal groups (Kellehear, 1993; Minichiello *et al.*, 1995). Human beings use body language and gaze (eye movements), either consciously or unconsciously, to convey various information such as emotion, social status or interest in interaction (Emmison and Smith, 2000). The relevance of recording non-verbal information in this study was an important consideration as children belong to the less literate and less verbal group. This is a feature that defines childhood and must therefore be a consideration in any research involving children. In addition, non-verbal ways of communication are an important aspect of children's language, and allowance needed to be made to include such language. The visual images 'allow researchers to discover previously unnoticed or ignored aspects of a scene or portrayal' (Kellehear, 1993, p.73). The distinct advantage of the audio-visual record is that it is available for re-analysis and re-checking, which promotes validity and reliability in qualitative research (Emmison and Smith, 2000). In our research the audio-visual record was extremely significant as analysis showed up many features of the children's expressions that would have been missed had we relied on the audio record alone (especially at times when their voices were inaudible).

Analysis and coding of verbal and non-verbal data

The analysis of qualitative data is inductive as 'categories, themes, and patterns come from the data and are not determined prior to the collection of the data' (Janesick, 2000, p.389). The researcher has to find the best way to tell the story and staying close to the data is the most powerful way to do this (Janesick, 2000; Neuman, 1997). The explanations or generalizations are more than simple descriptions, they are 'rich in detail, sensitive to context' (Neuman, 1997, p.420). Qualitative analysis requires the researcher to adopt a flexible, less pre-planned and less controlled approach to research, to listen and let the information speak for itself (Strauss and Corbin, 1998). Analysis of the non-verbal data was undertaken using the conversation analysis process. This seeks to remain faithful to the participant's perspectives and focuses specifically on the words and actions of the participants (Psathas, 1995). The process provides for the analysis of the various components of non-verbal language such as voice tone, body language and eye movements. It promotes analysis of such non-verbal language by the way it transcribes these interactions (see Hutchby and Wooffitt, 1998; Psathas, 1990, 1995).

Reliability and validity issues

Establishing the credibility of qualitative research is a problem constantly faced by qualitative researchers (Flick, 1998). Reliability, which specifies the stability of measurements, observations or results over time or settings, or methods which lead to this stability is one criterion for assessing qualitative research. The second criterion is validity, which refers to the validation of findings through replication (Padgett, 1998). Qualitative research, however, is about capturing the lived experiences and stories of individuals. The individual is not 'inserted' into the study but 'is the backbone of the study' (Janesick, 2000, p.393). In this study, the children were the primary focus and their experiences of abuse, as described by them, the essence. This type of qualitative research does not claim to be replicable nor objective. In fact, control of the research situation is purposefully avoided. In our research, a concerted effort was made to ensure as little influence as possible, over the voices of the children who participated in this research. They were encouraged to express their views in whatever way they chose.

There are, however, some criteria for checking the soundness of the study. These include clear explanation of the method so that the reader can judge whether it was adequate. Assumptions and biases are expressed, and the report acknowledges the limitations of generalizing the findings (Marshall and Rossman, 1995). The presence of the researcher over time in the field of study also ameliorates the effects of researcher reactivity and respondent bias (Padgett, 1998). It promotes trustworthiness, credibility and dependability (Flick, 1998). This was particularly relevant in our study as this was our chosen field of work from which the need for the research arose. Methods for checking the data, which are forms of validity checks (Flick, 1998; Minichiello et al., 1995), included the children being allowed to review their video-taped interviews at a separate time when they were allowed to add to or delete information from the interviews. Another check for validity is the volume and detail that is recorded from the research (Neuman, 1997) such as the direct quotes from the research participants presented in this book.

Problems and pitfalls encountered in this research

There were several problems that were encountered while undertaking this research. Some of these had been anticipated, but others became evident later. We suggest that these need to be considered in any future research with children who have been abused.

Impact of the topic on researchers

An issue that became apparent at the time of conducting the research interviews was the impact on the primary author of listening to the children's accounts of their experiences of abuse. Despite many years of professional clinical experience in providing therapy to children who had been abused, the narratives in the research interviews were deeply moving. They had a major emotional impact on the primary author at different stages of the research process. These stages were: during the research interviews, at review of the transcripts and the video-tapes, at the writing-up stage in the chapters that presented the results of the study, and at presentations of the findings to various audiences. It is important to note that any research on the topic of child abuse that attempts to present the voices of children who have been abused is likely to have a significant impact on the researcher. Opportunities to debrief at various times must therefore be built into the process.

The role of a counsellor versus that of a researcher

In an effort to remain objective and not influence any part of the child's narrative, the primary author was of the view that keeping a researcher role would be most appropriate during the research interview. However, the difference between the role of a researcher and that of a counsellor is not always clear. This created some obstacles. For example, when children seemed distressed during the interview, the primary author was often uncertain at what point to intervene without entirely disrupting their narratives and influencing the research process. Christensen (2004) draws attention to the need to reflect on the type of data likely to be produced if one focuses only on the research process. According to Calam and Franchi (1987) there is tension between the role of researcher and therapist. The relationship between client and professional influences the client towards change, which is central to the therapeutic process. In research, however, it requires restraint and restriction of behaviour on behalf of the researcher, in order to avoid bias. The researcher 'therefore cannot deal with issues as they arise in the research interview' (Calam and Franchi, 1987, p.183). As the interview was not a therapeutic session, the primary author had to consciously refrain from helping children process some of the traumatic events they were describing. While the child was debriefed at the close of the research interview, the primary author felt uncomfortable with the distress engendered by the research interview that had to be tolerated during the interview.

The issue of whether the researcher versus counsellor role can be entirely separated in research that involves children who have been abused is one that is not easy to resolve. Some views expressed by colleagues and fellow researchers are that this role cannot and should not be differentiated. Others believe that a counselling role can have a significant influence on the research interview and the research data. This is an issue that needs further exploration. Some clear guidelines may need to be established to guide future research with children who have been abused.

CHAPTER 6

Children's Voices

Their Views on Abuse and the Impact of Abuse

> How the abuse...has changed me? I think what happens with most kids is they grow up so quick. I had to grow up too quickly and I just feel like I missed out on childhood pretty much. ...you have to grow up pretty fast in that sort of situation, otherwise you don't survive. It's as simple as that.
>
> 18-year-old female

Introduction

Hearing directly from children who have been abused validates indirect sources on the process of victimization. In a report on a five-year-study of 2384 children referred for possible sexual abuse, Heger *et al.* state that history 'from the child remains the single most important diagnostic feature in coming to the conclusion that a child has been sexually abused' (2002, p.645). Our research supports this view and demonstrated that children do have the ability to eloquently describe their experiences of abuse and professional interventions.

This chapter presents children's voices about their experiences of abuse, why they believe children are abused, and their views on the impact of that abuse on them. The quotes and extracts have been taken directly from the research interviews where children chose to speak on these topics. Therefore, they do not represent the experiences of all the children who participated in our research.

Why children are abused

The following extracts demonstrate children's remarkable insight into the causes of abuse. Some clearly related the cause to the intergenerational transmission of abuse, as expressed in the following extract:

> I think…I sort of feel that with a lot of people it's the way they've been treated by their parents, and their parents being treated by their children, and it's just, because they've had it done to them they lash out on other people because, like, they don't know any way to channel their anger, because their parents or their parents' parents have lashed out on them and they don't know how else to express their anger because that's how they've been shown, that's how they've seen it. (12-year-old female)

A 13-year-old boy talked about the cycle of abuse, relating the abusive behaviour to an adult's experience of abuse in childhood and that adult not having made a disclosure:

> sometimes people do it to children because sometimes something might have happened to them. If it happened to them? I sort of feel sorry in a way, but then I say to myself, well, they shouldn't have did that in the first place. Now, the reason why that happened is because he [the child] didn't say anything about it when he was young…you know, they should tell someone… (13-year-old male)

It is interesting to note that some children had a clear view that the abuse of children had to do with abusers having control over younger, smaller people:

> Well, they're picking on people who are smaller than them. You know how they say with boys they are always bigger than you and they pick on you because you're smaller than them? I think it's just something like that, because I mean, D [abuser] was a grown man, J's [teenage abuser], like, she's three years older than me…[they] pick on people who are smaller than them and weaker than them, but in the end they're [the children], they're taller and they're stronger than them in the end. (11-year-old female)

> The other kids who do it or adults who do it to you they know it's wrong to, they know it's wrong, but they just, I don't know, makes you feel big or something, I'm not sure. (12-year-old male)

Some children's explanations for the sexual abuse of children portray their confusion about love and sex:

> That question was asked in group once and I got my hand slapped for my answer. Well, we were talking about whether it's an act of love or whether

love's involved, and I said I thought maybe it was. Like sort of with Dad it's just too much affection, and I was told off for that one. But I was kind of pissed off about that because if that's the belief I want to have, well I didn't want that taken away. I just feel it's a fixation he has on me not on others. I feel very strongly about that. (18-year-old female)

An 11-year-old girl voiced a similar sentiment, saying that the reason her grandfather had sexually abused her was because 'Yeah, he's over-affectionate [with me]'. She also talked about how familial access to children facilitates abuse:

That's probably because I was the closest one and probably the same thing with my grandfather, because I was the easiest target. It's like, it would be too difficult to go out into a shopping centre or something and catch whoever comes into the toilet or something and I was there at the time. (11-year-old female)

Other children saw their cognitive and physical incompetence as reasons for the abuse of children:

Because kids are more smaller, and kids can't fight back when they are young. You know, so…nasty people do that…that kind of stuff to kids. (13-year-old male)

Another 12-year-old boy said that children are 'not smart enough to know what's happening, like, they're not old enough to know it's, like, wrong to do it'. He went on to say that children under ten years old are more likely to be abused:

but, um, you don't see it very much happening to people, like, over 11 and 12 and that… Because they know about it and, like, they're a bit stronger than what they were when they were, like, young. (12-year-old male)

An 11-year-old girl was also quite clear that the reason she had been abused by her grandfather and father was 'Probably because I was that young and did not know what it was.'

Another 11-year-old girl felt it was the abuser's inability to cope with his life:

Because he, he can't, like, why he did it was probably because he can't cope with life and he needs something to help and… Yeah, he needed help, so he made someone else need help even worse. Like, maybe not even worse, but, yeah… (11-year-old female)

This 12-year-old girl supports this view:

> Probably similar to things with drugs, sort of, like, um, they can't have control over anything…that there's this little kid who just doesn't have anything, any control really over their life yet… I was frightened anyway. (12-year-old female)

The sadness and confusion about understanding the abuse by one's father is clearly verbalized by this 18-year-old young person who had been abused since infancy:

> I mean, in Dad's case I don't know, I don't know why… It's not something that I want to think about. (18-year-old female)

Finally, this 11-year-old girl clarifies why it is so difficult for children to protect themselves from abuse:

> Well, the problem is you don't know beforehand you don't know really what's going to happen or anything in the future. I mean, if it hadn't happened to you before or something then you just don't know…you don't really know why it is happening until you go to counselling. (11-year-old female)

Stories of abuse

Abuse: it's just very normal…

Growing up with abuse as part of one's life can be a bewildering and confusing experience for a child who has no option but to think that this is how families are supposed to be. This 18-year-old female describes her view of her life prior to her disclosure of sexual abuse by her father from infancy:

> Things were very normal for me. I saw things as being very normal. I didn't know any differently. I mean I wasn't ecstatic with life but there weren't any disruptions, I was just going along with it… It was just like washing the dishes or taking the dog for a walk. The abuse just slotted into it all. (18-year-old female)

An 11-year-old female describes the emotional impact on her of being rejected by her father who has had no contact with her since infancy:

> I've had to go through my whole life without a father there, my dad doesn't live with us, he doesn't care about me. I'm used to it, that's all I can say, I'm used to it. (11-year-old female)

Family violence: keeping the family secret safe

The opportunity to escape dangerous and frightening situations is diminished when children grow up in a home where violence is a common occurrence. Their fear, coupled with shame, promotes the need to keep the violence a secret, and prevents children from accessing outside support and help.

The following extract from a nine-year-old male describes his response to the violence in his home:

> *Researcher*: Did you used to go anywhere sometimes when things got difficult at home, like when there were lots of fights between Mum and Dad?
>
> *Nine-year-old male*: Um, no, I usually stayed home…um, I usually stayed in bed and listened til it went [quiet]…and then I went to sleep again.

In the popular novel, *Paddy Clarke Ha Ha Ha* (Doyle, 1993), the author describes the reaction of ten-year-old Paddy to his parents' fights and describes how he stays awake at night. He believes that if he can stay awake that would stop them fighting.

This is the impact of parental conflict on children in a relatively normal home where there is no abuse. It describes how alert and observant children are to the tensions in the home and their helplessness to intervene.

For an 11-year-old girl, the violence was more pervasive. She described how her life was different since she and her mother had moved away from her stepfather:

> Well probably because, you know, there's not going to be yelling and screaming down the other end of the house every night and, um, just because you don't have somebody coming up and belting you for just laying there trying to get to sleep. (11-year-old female)

A 13-year-old male, who was three or four years old when the violence by his mother's partner began, describes the frightening reality of such experiences:

> my life went bad and you know, this S [abuser], this mean devil used to be nasty to me all the time, used to bash my mum up, and you know, like you see your mum get bashed up and you almost got killed once, and you know, so you know you are not a normal, you wouldn't be a normal person if you are going through something like that. (13-year-old male)

The violence ranged in degree and frequency. The following are some descriptions of the violence that the children experienced. This nine-year-old male talked about his father's violence:

> Um, I remember one of their fights and that wasn't a good one... My dad used...used his feet. He pushed Mum over with it. (9-year-old male)

An 11-year-old boy described his experience of violence as follows:

> It didn't happen every day, it only happened at night usually...Dad used to punch holes everywhere. (11-year-old male)

For this 11-year-old girl, the violence was directed at both her and her mother:

> Um, when this happened to Mum I was with my nanna or something, ...he actually went and he hit Mum in the head and she ended up with this massive bruise... And then, he started building this extension, an en suite extension, and...oh, I was holding a plank of wood, because he was doing it himself basically, he's cutting a plank of wood and he reckoned I moved it, and he came over, he said I moved it, and I hadn't even moved it, he came over and he grabbed me like that and he shoved me across the room and as he did that his fist went into the side of my head and it hurt... I felt like he was going to hit me again or something. I was just, I was scared, I thought he was going to belt me again or bash me up or something. (11-year-old female)

She goes on to describe what she believes would have happened if she had not disclosed the abuse:

> Well, [we'd] probably still be with D and Mum and probably somebody would get seriously hurt by now, somebody would've, could have even died or something by now. (11-year-old female)

Sexual abuse: 'I hated what he did' (13-year-old male)

Sexual abuse is the 'ultimate betrayal' (Forward, 1989, p.138). It has devastating emotional effects because 'the young victims...have nowhere to run, no one to run to. Protectors become persecutors, and reality becomes a prison of dirty secrets' (Forward, 1989, p.138).

The following extracts demonstrate how some children experienced sexual abuse. This 18-year-old female talks about her superficial disclosures to a school counsellor:

> No, I'd only talked to her about the um, the lack of privacy and whatever, basic stuff like, I don't know, like Dad coming in when I was getting changed or in the bath or the shower or whatever. But I didn't tell her about anything else at the time. So we were just working on that and the fact that I felt uncomfortable. (18-year-old female)

An 11-year-old girl described how she experienced the sexual abuse by her maternal grandfather and later by her father as different:

> um, with my grandfather that went on for longer, but with my dad it was only like pretty short, but with my dad I thought it was really hard. (11-year-old female)

For a 13-year-old boy the sexual abuse by his mother's partner began after many years of extreme violence both to him and his mother. The quotation below demonstrates how difficult it was for him to verbalize the sexual abuse:

> Mmmm. I hated what he did. Yeah, well what he did to me, is that...umm...one day, Christ...one day, I was in the bath, and um, he was washing me...and um, he sort of...um, did something what he shouldn't have done...and I think you already know what, you know...I was about, oh, about seven, you know, I know people bath, bath ya, but like, when you bath somebody, you don't play with people, and I didn't know that, because he covered my mouth so I couldn't talk, and then he...did...you know...you know, that's it... (13-year-old male)

For this boy, the violence and sexual abuse also had elements of ritual abuse:

> Um, he used to chain me up in the er...garage, and used to tie me up with sticky tape and I used to be completely naked for about three to four hours hanging up in the room... He used to cut me, or it is like, I don't know, some f—ing voodoo thing... (13-year-old male)

The effects of abuse: abuse hurts

'It just creeps into every part of your life' (18-year-old female)

Some authors suggest that the emotional and behavioural changes in abused children are their attempts to adapt to their environment, which includes the abuse. It is therefore not a symptom but a response to protecting themselves at that time (Hanks and Stratton, 1995). Hanks and Stratton therefore see the consequences of abuse as adaptations by the child to cope with the abuse, the 'adaptation the child is forced into' (p.90). Accommodating ongoing abuse involves developing behaviours 'to increase safety and/or decrease pain during victimisation' (Briere, 1992, p.17). Briere goes on to say that the link between child abuse and dysfunctional behaviour has been disregarded and minimized. In this section, the children describe a range of behaviours they displayed in response to living with the secret of the abuse.

Short-term impact: behavioural issues

This 12-year-old boy describes his behaviour prior to disclosing the abuse:

> Umm... Well, I was like really getting into them [my parents], like, not physically but, like, verbally, like yelling out and swearing at them and then they didn't know why, and then after a while I think I told Mum first and then she told Dad what happened, and then Dad rang the policeman down the road. (12-year-old male)

Many children were able to identify that their behaviour had changed in response to the abuse:

> I was just a...I used to be...I have a high temper, used to throw chairs around the room and used to be like a wild tornado. (13-year-old male)

Similarly this 12-year-old boy describes his aggressive behaviour at school:

> Umm... Oh, we were looking for places [for counselling] because my attitude at school was really changing; like, I was getting in a lot of trouble, getting in all these fights and that... Well, if someone said just one thing to me...if someone said like one word I'd be hitting him, yeah. (12-year-old male)

This 18-year-old young girl, on the other hand, seems to demonstrate the gender differences in coping behaviours between males and females with males displaying aggressive, acting-out behaviours while she became more introverted and withdrawn:

> Well, my parents sent me off to a school counsellor in Year 7, I think it was...I think it's because I'm so sort of quiet and didn't have loads of friends hanging off my arms, so they sent me along to the school counsellor. (18-year-old female)

Suicidal and self-destructive behaviours are also more common among female victims, who look for various ways to express the fear and anxiety

within them. The following extracts describe the various self-destructive behaviours used by these girls:

> Because, um…I didn't have any control over my life then so I started
> controlling my food, I would either eat it and throw it up again, or I just
> wouldn't eat. (11-year-old female)

> Well, I think before it all became an issue, my coping strategies were sort
> of at subconscious levels so I wasn't aware of it, but I was over listening.
> Whereas now, or when it all sort of hit the fan, you know I had to develop
> some new ways…turned to ways of denying all the pain and the issues
> and whatever…I went through a stage with drinking and the drugs and
> that didn't particularly help. I was a great one for the old self-mutilation
> as well. (18-year-old female)

> [B]ecause I lose my temper a lot too and I'm here [at counselling] because
> I'm seeing other ways to control my temper and that… I have actually
> thought about killing myself before. (12-year-old female)

Long-term impact: emotional and psychological issues: it will never go away…

Many of the children seemed to understand that the impact of the abuse
would remain with them for the rest of their lives:

> Probably, I think it will be there really the rest of my life, but, when I'm,
> like, doing something it's probably the last thing on my mind. …like, I
> don't really like remember the stuff but…if someone says something I
> know, then I think about what happened… (12-year-old male)

> You can't forget something like that. I'll still be dealing with things later
> down the track. It's always going to be in the back of your mind. I don't
> think it will ever go away. (18-year-old female)

Some writers have suggested that one of the consequences of extreme childhood abuse may be the development of a dissociative coping style (Herman,
1992; Irwin, 1998). Dissociation is described as an alteration to a person's
identity where the usual identity is temporarily forgotten and a new one is
assumed or imposed (Briere, 1992). This 13-year-old male describes how he
imposed a new and more powerful identity from the movie and video game
(*Mortal Kombat*) to cope with the abuse:

> OK… When I am Scorpion, well I am Scorpion, like I am more powerful
> than what I am, and I'm like an immortal now, because like, everything of

> me has been put back in, but I haven't got a... M [child's name] hasn't got a soul, M is dead, because he got destroyed, and M's soul got destroyed and so, but I am Scorpion, I am 100 per cent Scorpion. (13-year-old male)

Some children clearly described that they believed they and their lives would have been different had the abuse not happened:

> I wouldn't be worrying about that the whole time and when – oh, how can I explain, I wouldn't be worrying about it the whole time. I wouldn't like watch if it was on TV...it wouldn't have upset me if I didn't know what it really meant, but now I do. (12-year-old male)

> Well, I'd probably be at...[name of university] Uni doing medicine, a most outgoing, happy, lively person you'd ever met... I don't know, it's just so hard... (18-year-old female)

> Um, probably I would just be normal and I wouldn't need all the counselling and that. (11-year-old female)

Becoming stronger: I wish it happened a different way...

Despite awareness of the negative impact of the abuse on their lives, some children were able to admit that they had grown as a result of the experience:

> Um, now I know about this stuff, like – I didn't want to find out this way but I know a lot by Mum talking to me about it. [I feel] stronger in a way because now if it comes across me again I know what to do, I know. (12-year-old male)

This 11-year-old girl acknowledged that counselling helped her in more areas of her life than just the abuse. She has now found ways to deal with the teasing from kids at school and so acknowledges that had she not been abused, she would not have had access to counselling.

> Well, I guess kind of if O [grandfather] hadn't done that, my life would have been...sad, sadder than it is now, so I'm kind of peed off and kind of glad that O did, but I wish that my life had improved a better way than having to go through that. ...I mean, I think about bad things but I don't let them get to me, which I think is a good quality to have and I stick up for myself too... I had to, I had to toughen up, or I'd be an emotional wreck, literally, an emotional wreck. (11-year-old female)

Conclusion

While research seeking children's views is still relatively new (Amaya-Jackson *et al.*, 2000), this research has suggested that, given the opportunity, children have the capacity to voice their views about matters that affect them. In fact, despite their perceived cognitive and emotional limitations, the voices of children provide compelling insights and understandings about the dynamics of abuse. As Mauthner states, 'when space is made for them, children's voices express themselves clearly' (1997, p.21). Current information and research from the literature on child abuse can therefore find powerful support from listening to children describe their own experiences of victimization.

CHAPTER 7

Children's Voices
Their Views about Making Disclosures, about Abusers and Non-offending Parents

[I felt] frightened, very, very frightened and…and trust me, it's very, very
scary.

11-year-old female

Introduction: to tell or not to tell

A disclosure of abuse by a child is often the first step in the child protection
process. Often major decisions are based on the outcome of interviews with
children where a suspicion of abuse exists. Yet little is known about how
children think and feel about making disclosures of abuse. The following
extracts demonstrate how complex it is for children to reveal abuse. They
provide insight into children's thoughts and anxieties, and their decisions
about disclosing the abuse.

This young boy talks about how hesitant and unsure he was about
whether to tell his parents about the abuse:

> I did, but I didn't, like, want to tell. I wanted to but I didn't, like, want to,
> do you know what I mean? …I was thinking, if I told and he found out, I
> would be in serious trouble or if I didn't tell I would just have this kept in
> my mind. So I went and told my mum and then she said to tell Dad
> (13-year-old male)

For this 18-year-old female, she felt her decision not to disclose the full
details of her father's abuse of her was appropriate. Her mother was supportive of her until she disclosed further details of the abuse:

> I think to a degree it was a conscious decision, I guess I was testing the waters and it proved to be a good thing because for starters, Mum had great difficulty understanding the few things that I sort of tried to bring to her attention. So, if I sort of said, well…Dad's done this, this, this and this, then there'd be no chance, so I guess also when Community Services [the protective services department] became involved I really didn't tell them that great a deal because I didn't know what they were going to do. (18-year-old female)

The following quotation demonstrates the various factors a child may consider as part of making a disclosure of abuse:

> because I mean, like, like, with the thing with J [teenage abuser] I didn't speak out about that until a year after we'd moved. Like, when we moved I was nine. I didn't tell until I was 11. Well, probably just because some things like that are embarrassing and because people hadn't believed me… (12-year-old female)

This 11-year-old girl talks about the reality of threats made by abusers:

> Sometimes because what happened to me, they threatened me, if you don't do this I'll do this to you or something. It is hard to [tell]…though. I don't know, I thought – um…the thing was when I was five, I thought, well if no one's going to help me I may as well tell somebody so that they can help me, because Mum doesn't seem to know. (11-year-old female)

Sometimes the pressure of keeping the secret of abuse becomes too much for a child:

> Well, I only told one person in my family, which was Mum…and what happened was I was crying in the morning, really, really badly crying…and so Mum didn't make me go to school…when I was crying so badly, which is very nice of her, I've got a good Mum all in all. And anyway, so I didn't go to school and, um, that's when I told Mum about it which took me a lot of thinking to remember…because I can't remember it well enough, there's so much else… [I felt] frightened, very, very frightened and I guess I was seven or eight then, and…and trust me, it's very, very scary. (11-year-old female)

This girl also talked about the importance of not forcing children into making a disclosure and this is what she appreciated about her mother:

she [mother] helped by not making me, not rushing me to get it out, which, um, I think it's a really stupid idea to make kids get it out A.S.A.P. (11-year-old female)

Facilitating disclosures: so that's *what's happening!*

This 11-year-old girl said she was worried about what would happen to her father and therefore could not disclose while he lived with them. She found it easier to disclose the abuse by him after her mother chose to get a divorce. She also felt that parents who have had some experience of abuse would be able to read the signs in their children and facilitate disclosures:

> It would probably be easier for parents who have had that sort of experience because they sort of notice your moods and they sort of relate to it and then they sort of, because Mum did notice that. She was trying to put a finger on it but she just couldn't and then one day she put a finger on it and that same day I told her, so she went, oh, that's what's happening. (11-year-old female)

Another 11-year-old girl mentioned her anxiety about making disclosures to males even though the person may be her father or a father figure.

> I'd like Mum to know actually, but I wouldn't like R [mother's partner] or Dad to know, because I'm a girl and I say girl's things…

Post-disclosure: the pain is still there…

Some children talked about the emotional impact of abuse, which persists well after the disclosure of abuse:

> The first part was bad. Actually the whole day the feeling was bad but it was also good because I got it out and something was getting done about it. So that was why it was good and bad, but I was pretty sad actually. A lot of the times I am actually sad but I don't know why. (11-year-old female)

> Well, I found a huge issue for me is that for a while it's all out in the open you get endless amounts of support, everyone's there for you, but after a while, you know everyone kind of forgets, but you still carry the pain, it's not necessarily any less. I really wish people were aware of that. (18-year-old female)

This 18-year-old young person goes on to describe what impact her disclosure had on her relationship with her father and, despite his abuse of her, she feels sad at not being able to regain this relationship:

> Oh, we've always had a pretty rocky relationship, we've always sort of been at each other, stirring each other. Yeah we had a pretty good relationship, we had a lot of good times together. Makes it a bit difficult now... Because like I keep saying, everything was normal to me back then so, it was great. There was no tension between the two of us, there was no, sort of none of the bullshit that goes on now. So...it's screwed things up completely. (18-year-old female)

Threats related to disclosures: if you tell...

For several children, apart from their own emotional fears and concerns about disclosing the abuse, abusers often made threats to prevent the children from letting out the secret of the abuse. The following extracts demonstrate some of the threats the children experienced. Some abusers used threats of violence:

> He threatened to beat me up if like I, if I, um, I didn't do what he said or if I told anyone, he'd really get me then...then I didn't tell anyone for, I think it was a year, half a year, or...I'm not sure. (12-year-old male)

> M'mm. Like, she [teenage abuser] was denying it and with what it was, she always used to threaten that if I didn't do it, like E [younger sibling] is small, for a five-year-old she's a petite person and she [teenage abuser] always used to say she'd break her arms and everything...and I didn't know what to do... (12-year-old female)

For this 11-year-old girl her father used a more invidious way to prevent her disclosure in comparison to her grandfather:

> Um, with my grandfather, it was, um, um, a rusty nail through my hand and with my dad he knew I didn't like Mum and Dad fighting because, um, um he threatened that they'd fight and that was enough to make me shut up. [It was] very scary and very confused, like, very scared and very confused. You've got all this fear and confusion and stuff inside you and you want to let it out but you know you shouldn't because of all these threats that are on you. (11-year-old female)

Children speak: children's views of the abuser

This section provides a glimpse into the thoughts of children about abusers. It demonstrates their confusion when the abuser is part of the family.

Before it all happened...

Some children described the abuser as being nice before the abuse began:

> I don't know, we were friends, like every day when I came down to the basketball court he came out and played basketball... (12-year-old male)

> Yeah, he [grandfather] was actually [nice], except he smoked and when I sat on his lap he smoked and drank and the smoke got in my face...he's over-affectionate [with me]. (11-year-old female)

> [H]e used to be a really nice person, he was a loving person, before he had a stroke. He tripped over and knocked himself out, went to the hospital, four weeks later he had a stroke and he started chucking a fit, and then he was a bastard. He went mad...he was f—ing mental. (13-year-old male)

> I know he [father] does love me, I know he loves me a heck of a lot, and I always just figured it was just over fondness or something...the thing that people don't understand is that yes, your dad may abuse you or your mother or whatever, but you still love them, you still have feelings for them, they're still your parents and you don't want to lose them. (18-year-old female)

Why they did it...

Children had various views about why abusers choose to abuse them and, for some, it was difficult to understand why abuse happened:

> I mean in Dad's case, I don't [know] why. It's not something I want to think about. Go with the flow and accept it. If you're looking for answers, you're not going to get it. I mean, I don't know if it would make much, that much difference to me if I knew why. (18-year-old female)

Some children felt that the abusive behaviour was just the way a person was:

> I'm not sure, just do his block, just do his block a bit...that was his way. (9-year-old male)

His older brother, however, felt it was because of his father's drinking:

> Yep, went to the pub too much…because he used to play cricket. (11-year-old male)

This girl shows insight in her description of why people abuse children:

> They've got a problem… Um, a problem that…umm, they want something but they can't really have it and they sort of want control over something because they don't have control over their life. (11-year-old female)

For this 18-year-old young girl, on the other hand, she describes her father as persistent in his abusive behaviour:

> [He's] a trier, doesn't give up. He just keeps going, just keeps pushing. (18-year-old female)

Some children were unable to suppress the anger and fear they felt towards the abuser:

> The devil, that is S [abuser]. He is like, to me, like Satan's son, because he just acts like him because he is evil and so I call him the devil instead. I used to think he was an animal, but a bloody animal wouldn't even do that, an animal don't bash their own up. He hated me. He said he was going to kill me anyway. (13-year-old male)

This boy talks about how difficult it is to know who may be an abuser:

> I don't know…you can't like really suspect, like, oh yeah…they're the ones that are bad inside, but it's just like they're corny, you know, and sometimes, like, you don't know what to do really. (13-year-old male)

Consequences for abusing

The research explored children's views on how abusers should be responded to. It was interesting to note that many children differentiated between consequences for their fathers as against other abusers, including grandparents.

FATHERS

> It is a bit harder with Dad, though, because he's my dad and I know he did that sort of thing to me, but it's a bit harder. I'm not sure. If I had my way…a couple of years of community services. Because I don't want him to go to jail because he's my dad, but I want him to get punished for what he did and I want to put in a realistic point of view. (11-year-old female)

Another girl had a similar view but also felt responsible for the consequences of her disclosure and the resultant disruption to her family:

> I think they should go through months and years of counselling. But I guess that's not going to help them if they don't see that it's an issue, it would just be wasted time wouldn't it? I mean, when I think about my dad and what I've done to him, I don't want him put in jail or anything like that, so, I don't know. (18-year-old female)

GRANDFATHERS

How grandfathers should be responded to for abusing them provoked a range of interesting suggestions, as the following extracts demonstrate:

> Well, a, no not a taste of his own medicine, because I don't think that's appropriate. If I had to say, well actually...I would seriously chuck a tantrum at him, I might even whack him. I'd tell him how cruel he was, how dumb he is and how mean he is and how stupid. What I think should be done is he should have a good talking to and maybe have to live on his own, be on his own and not see anyone, so be away from everyone, every single person, never ever to see a living soul again. I think that's what should happen. That would be pretty cool if that happened because then I could go and see Nanna in her house. (11-year-old female)

> Well, um, I know they can't really put everybody in jail, but, like, if my grandfather did it to two people I think that they should have at least taken him to court or something. ...find some way to give him a bug or something, send him to Africa or something, let them die a slow way and a peaceful death. I know that doesn't sound very nice, but that's what I think. (12-year-old female)

OTHER ABUSERS

Similarly children had definite ideas about how their abusers should be responded to. Nearly all of them felt that there should be consequences. This boy expresses shock at the minimal jail sentence his abuser received:

> I wish he was f—ing, well, he should be dead for what he did. He should suffer for what he has done, and he hasn't. Six months in jail! That, that was good in a way, because that six months got us enough time to piss off, but still, he could have got more. (13-year-old male)

Another boy, who had been abused by a male peer, suggested a children's jail for his abuser:

> Oh, he should, should have been, should have been put in jail. You'd grab them and put them in jail and they can't do it any more…and they should make a children's jail. (12-year-old male)

While jail was an option that some considered, others saw counselling as important. One girl was convinced that counselling was the best option. She felt her own counselling had helped her, and that therefore her mother's partner and his daughter, both of whom had abused her, should have access to counselling services:

> I reckon if you ask me what my opinion would be, that if the courts would listen I reckon there should have to be, like, some sort of counselling for what they've done because, I mean, like, with P [mother's partner] it is probably not the first time he's done it. 'Cos I mean like J [teenage abuser], she needs help and so does P. If he, if he doesn't get his way he just totally loses his temper and he needs someone to talk to, to be able to channel [his anger]. …and that's what I'm doing as well, because I lose my temper a lot too and…I'm seeing other ways to control my temper. (12 year old female)

This boy, however, expressed very strong anger and a desire to totally destroy the abuser:

> You know what I wouldn't mind doing, with S? Putting him and butchering him like a bloody, no that's not fair to an animal – but be slaughtered, like the old days, you know, do what them used to do, you know, a long time ago. Because if you ask me, I reckon that is the most painfullest way to be killed, is to be slaughtered like an animal…then you know what I would do with the remains of him? I would get the remains of him and I would put them in a big cardboard box and you know what I would do then? Get TNT and bloody blow the whole flaming box up in the pits, then I would get his skull and then I would hang it up on the wall as a little mantelpiece. (13-year-old male)

He had similar views on what should happen to people who abuse children:

> Get the living shit shot out of them, or get in a pool of sharks and see him get ripped into little bits and pieces, I sound like a criminal the way I am talkin', but you know, that is what I reckon should happen to people, nasty people that do that kind of stuff to kids. (13-year-old male)

This girl concludes with a strong message to abusers:

Those people that abuse children or think about abusing children, go get stuffed. (11-year-old female)

Section summary

This section presented in some detail children's views of the abuser. Most children were able to identify that there had been a positive relationship with the abuser prior to the abuse. For several who had been abused by their fathers, the complexity of the issue becomes apparent. Many talked about the difficulty associated with not wanting to break up their families, not wanting their fathers to be punished severely, and the fact that they loved their fathers. Many children also demonstrated insight into the reasons that people abuse children, verbalizing common theoretical positions on the causes of child abuse.

Children speak: children's views of the non-offending parent(s)

Child abuse has a major impact on other family members as well. The emotional impact on the non-offending parent can be so extreme as to render them helpless and/or unavailable to their child (Tower, 1989). Physical consequences, too, such as having to make a decision to separate from the offending parent, may cause a major family crisis. Often, the consequences for the whole family depend on the reactions of the non-offending parent (MacFarlane, Cockriel and Dugan, 1990). Sometimes the reaction of this parent to disclosures of abuse can have an impact that may be experienced by the child as worse than the abuse. Children may fail to disclose abuse out of fear that they may be punished (Summit, 1983) or may harbour a fear that a parent's anger at the abuser may result in a confrontation with the abuser, which children find particularly frightening.

Mothers

Most of the children who participated in the research had made their initial disclosures to their mothers. However they received mixed responses from them. Some of them felt fully supported and believed by their mothers. Others, however, experienced less positive responses. The following extracts demonstrate how children felt about the disclosures to their mothers. For some children, it is evident that the mother is the primary carer:

I've probably told Mum more things than I have to Dad, because, like, Mum's around more and, like, she's there when I need, because Dad, like, he's mostly at work and when he comes home, like, he's a good dad and that, er… but Mum's always around. When I'm sick she picks me up from school. She still has a job and everything, if I'm really sick, like throwing up all over the school, she comes and picks me up straight away. (13-year-old male)

Mum was very good and helped by not making me, not rushing me to get it out…Mum's very, very understanding about it…but, I mean, I guess every kid thinks their mum's the best, well, not every kid, but a lot of kids. (11-year-old female)

Another girl also described that it is difficult for parents to understand their child's behaviour prior to disclosure if they have not had any experience of abuse:

because Mum did notice that [my behaviour], she was trying to put a finger on it but she just couldn't and then one day she put a finger on it and that same day I told her. (11-year-old female)

This boy found his mother inaccessible at times when he wanted to talk to her of the violence or the conflict in the home:

Nup, she was usually tired or something like that. (11-year-old male)

For another boy, he felt concerned for his mother but also describes his sadness at his mother's vulnerability to her partner's persuasive powers:

Mum was scared, Mum didn't know what to do…eventually I told Mum what he did…actually, there was one thing that I was nicked off with. I felt like I was let down with Mum, because, like she…you know, like she let herself get sucked in three times. (13-year-old male)

This 18-year-old female explains how her mother's response to her changed when she realized that she would not retract her disclosure. It demonstrates the importance of parental responses to children's disclosures:

Actually she [Mum] was freaking out too. Not because of what I'd said but the fact that this had all come out of the blue, and this was a big department that was going to come barging into their lives, into Mum and Dad's lives, so, that's how it all sort of started. …er, in the very early stages she was supportive in terms of she was very comforting towards me. …but um, as things got further down the track and she realized that I wasn't sort of saying none of this is not true, that it's all lies, I was just making it up, she turned away from me. There was a, she went through a phase where she was prepared to look at the fact that yes, I had been abused, but not by Dad. That's as good as it got…everything she did right from the start told me that she wasn't fully supporting me so. I was absolutely devastated. In a way it was worse than the abuse. The abuse I could handle, that was easy. This is something new and I'm just shattered…I feel very bitter towards her at times. (18-year-old female)

For some, the immediate response from their mothers confirmed that they were believed and that their safety was a priority:

As soon as I told Mum they separated, so… (11-year-old female)

Yeah, eventually I told Mum what he did. Mum rang up the police…and Mum said that – well, this person is going to do something naughty and…now he is going to be in trouble for what he has done. And that was it. I never seen him again. (13-year-old male)

When I told Mum I had somebody to back me up because Aunty had seen the bruise and all that. Unfortunately she didn't take a photo, and I wish she did now because it would have helped a bit, but…she [Mum] up and left after she found out. (12-year-old female)

Fathers

Some children who were supported by both parents said they were worried about an aggressive reaction from their father or their substitute father to their disclosure:

I'm scared that some things I tell Mum will get to B [mother's partner], and I think B is a good person – like I am scared of him because he's strong enough to do anything, but I know he won't hurt me, because he can lose his temper. One time he kicked the table, and I felt like running out of the room, he's scary but he means no harm and he won't hurt us, I know that, but okay if you knew how angry he was, boy would you be scared. Oh, I didn't want to tell because I thought that I might get into trouble. (11-year-old female)

This boy would prefer his father to be more supportive:

Well…he could have, he was caring but he could have been interested a bit more than what he was. He's still not, he's still, like, I love them both the same, but, like, Mum's there when I really need her. (12-year-old male)

What I would have liked from them...

Some children were able to verbalize how they would have wanted their parents to respond:

> Umm...sort of, umm, I don't know, just stay cool and that, like, yeah. Well, Mum was really supportive the whole way through, but she got a bit emotional sometimes and was really sad... I didn't want Mum to feel sad because that makes me sad when she's sad. (12-year-old male)

For this young girl, she was desperate to be believed. Her mother and family believed that the abuse was in her head, that she had made it all up. She wished her mother had supported her:

> It's pretty obvious that I'm not the headcase that everyone else thinks I am. I don't just make these things up for fun. You know, I don't know if that would have made things any easier if she'd taken my side. (18-year-old female)

Impact on parents

It was interesting to note that some children were able to acknowledge the impact their disclosure had had on their parents. They voiced their views as follows:

> Mmm... At the start, like, they've never, like, handled a situation like that before, but then once they started getting counselling themselves, like, it all worked out really, like, they started feeling much better, like, in themselves. (12-year-old male)

There is insight in this next extract into why this young person's mother found it difficult to believe her and the divided loyalty a mother must experience in having to choose who to believe – her child or her husband:

> Er...I often try and put myself in her shoes, it can't exactly be easy for her. This guy she married, has been married to for 25 years or something, you think you know each other inside out, and this comes up, it's pretty hard to accept, isn't it? And I'm just a teenager, a moody teenager, who happened to have a few bad experiences along the line so she just put it down to those. (18-year-old female)

Section summary

How children experienced the role of their non-offending parent(s) in relation to the abuse demonstrates a mixture of experiences. Some found their parent(s) extremely supportive and others felt let down by them. The role of the non-offending parent, however, is very significant and particularly important to children when abuse occurs.

CHAPTER 8

Children's Voices

Their Experience of Professional Interventions

The problem with these people is that... They don't want to hear the truth because the truth is so much harder to understand and so much longer than a lie about the truth.

12-year-old female

Introduction

How do children feel about the various professionals who are part of the child protection system and who may become involved when a child has been abused? These professionals may include child protection workers, police, counsellors (psychologists, psychiatrists or social workers, or family court counsellors), school counsellors and people working within the legal and court systems. Depending on the nature of the abuse and the particular family situation, any one of these professionals may be the first to become involved with the child and/or the family. The responses of these professionals may be different depending on their role within the child protection system. For example, a protective worker may focus on the protection and welfare of the child, while the police may be more concerned about collecting evidence for the prosecution of an offender.

This chapter presents children's views of how they experienced interventions by certain professionals.

General comments on professional interventions

Just not helpful

This 12-year-old girl believes that some professionals are not helpful, they find the truth too hard to deal with and they therefore tend to side with adults rather than listen to the child:

> The problem with Miss [children's court counsellor]...was she didn't want to believe the truth and that's always the problem with these people, they don't want to believe the truth, they just want to believe the easiest side, the side that is easiest to, that is the simplest, basically...so then they get paid and go on to the next one and just pick the simplest out of that. They don't want to hear the truth because the truth is so much harder to understand and so much longer than a lie about the truth. (12-year-old female)

She seems to have a definite view that a professional's role is to listen to a child:

> I mean, people like that are supposed to listen, they're not supposed to sit there and tell you what you're thinking or what you're feeling, because that's what she was doing, just sitting there and telling me what's right. (12-year-old female)

Another young person was also unhappy with the way the report was made to child protection services by a sexual assault counsellor. She felt unprepared, not consulted and overlooked:

> I just wished to hell that the girl that I was seeing took time to explain things to me...maybe speak to me first about what [child protection] was, why she wanted to contact them. Maybe we could have worked something out, rather than [for me] to just get this phone call out of the blue saying well, you know, someone else is involved now. (18-year-old female)

An 11-year-old boy said that the first counsellor he saw 'knew nothing':

> I had two [counsellors]; one before that was very, didn't know nothing. I forget the name...because it was like six years ago or something. She just didn't know much about counselling and all that. We'd talk about it and then she'd [say], righto, see you tomorrow, something like that. (11-year-old male)

I've heard it all before

This 18-year-old young person describes in some detail how important the response from a professional is when a child is talking about or disclosing details of abuse:

> Um, another huge problem I have…er…is…you know, you start talking about a particular abuse or incident that happened, it's something that you've never talked about and you know, it's painful and all that, and…it's huge for you to get it out and you just…you know, think oh shit, and the person at the other end goes, oh yeah, well okay, we're going to have to do this, this or that, and that's okay, we'll do whatever. I mean they just kind of treat you like they've heard this a million times before, they've become immune to hearing these sorts of things. (18-year-old female)

She makes it clear that responses that minimize the abuse are quite shattering:

> I think it's really important that, when I reveal some incident and they just sort of blow it off, or whatever, it feels like a kick in the teeth, like it's not that big an issue because they've heard bigger and worse this and that and whatever. It's so important no matter how many times you've heard that kind of thing happening, that you treat it like it's a first time. (18-year-old female)

She shows insight into the possibility that some professionals respond in this way to protect themselves from the pain of hearing disclosures:

> I mean, I understand that for a lot of people, sort of they step back from it because that might be their way of dealing with it without trying to let their feelings become involved or whatever, but at the same point, it's so important for the child to know that, well, this is something pretty horrific and that your feelings are valid. It's kind of like some people I've been to talk to, it's just like they've got a standard response for everything…I mean for me, I just wanted to know that people cared about me, I didn't want to hear all this sort of statistics and facts on abuse or anything like that. (18-year-old female)

He's too difficult to deal with

This 13-year-old boy felt that some professionals tend to reject children who are classified as too difficult to engage with:

> there was only a couple [of psychologists], but like, half of them were just stuffing me around, like all they wanted to do was just do their stupid, like a stupid, dumb job or something, but they didn't actually really care about me. It was just like…oh, you know, you know, he is too, you know…why don't we just forget about him? And…they didn't have to do that, you know, you don't do that to people. Well, in my book, you don't anyway. (13-year-old male)

Being believed

The importance of professionals believing children and letting them tell their story is eloquently verbalized by this 12-year-old girl who feels very angry at the reaction of this counsellor:

> It was weird, I didn't have a choice [about counselling]…it was ordered by the court. I didn't want to go 'cos I had people before who didn't believe me. Professional people have said, like I'm mentally unstable and that Mum's telling me all this stuff and it's all in my head. Well, we went to see this person…she started telling me, oh this happened and that didn't happen, and my mum could hear me from in the foyer crying, and here's me sitting in front of…and she just told me what's what…and that I wasn't abused and that all this in my head isn't real but my mum's been putting it in my head. She was telling me what I thought and I was just saying, that's not it. (12-year-old female)

Courts should 'have their bloody consideration right' and listen to kids

Some children believed that there should be an opportunity for courts to hear what children have to say. This boy is critical about the fact that the courts do not make provision to accommodate a child's testimony:

> because the courts didn't listen to me when I was young. They didn't even want to put me in court, you know, little do they know what happened to me, you know. You know, it is sort of unfair when you think about it, hey? (13-year-old male)

He is scathing about the inadequate response of the court to the abuser:

> As far as I am concerned, and sorry for saying this, but if you ask me…you know the system is well and truly stuffed. Because like, you know, he could just get married or something and do the same thing. Well, I reckon what should happen is that the umm, people in the courts

should have the bloody consideration and…I reckon us kids should have the right to be listened to, when or whenever we need to be helped, and when we are in danger. (13-year-old male)

He goes on to say that counsellors should be allowed to represent the child in court and that the legal system should make allowance for this:

Yeah, actually I reckon they should get, get the authority from the police…if you believe what the kid is saying, that the person who is actually doing it, can actually get charged straight away for what he has done. And the person, the counsellor should go to court with them [the child] and represent them to the judge and jury, and if the kid doesn't know exactly what to say – you know, tell him, make him say the main stuff, what has happened, and you know, and let the counsellor say the rest, because he or her [the child] starts getting too emotional. (13-year-old male)

Professionals come and go

Several children were seen by many different professionals:

Yeah, I had about a hundred of 'em, probably. No, not a hundred, but…yeah, a few. (13-year-old male)

Well, there was a whole range of agencies involved in this. Yeah, and between that time there's probably been four or five counsellors and probably psychiatrists that Mum and Dad sent me to. (18-year-old female)

A different kind of counsellor

This 11-year-old girl describes her first experience of a counsellor:

this counsellor had a Maltese terrier and she was actually more talking to Mum and Dad, but I was actually getting my own counselling with the dog, I was talking with the dog [laughs]. I had all my feelings bottled up into this box and I had to draw the box and then we burnt the picture and that sort of, it then sort of made me, well, sort of relieved. Which I know sounds really weird because I burnt this picture of something and it sort of made me a little bit better. (11-year-old female)

This 18-year-old young person viewed her experience with the school counsellor as very positive:

I built a pretty good friendship with her [the school counsellor]. Up until then I had never sort of talked to anyone about really anything, it was fantastic to have someone that I could go to talk to, and the thing is we didn't just talk about the yukky stuff, I could just go in there if I was feeling a bit down and we'd just talk about whatever, gardening, dogs, whatever. So, it was something. (18-year-old female)

Views about police involvement

While a major consideration of the police in child protection is the welfare of the child, the focus of their work is to ascertain whether a criminal offence has been committed. They seek to establish who the offender is, to gather evidence to determine if a conviction should be sought and 'if so, to maximize the likelihood of obtaining a conviction' (Sanders, 1999, p.197). However, their role in child abuse differs from community to community and sometimes between different states within a country (Tower, 1989). In some places they may have primary responsibility for taking reports and investigating allegations of child abuse, while in others their primary role may be to collect evidence for criminal charges against the abuser and be supportive to child protection services. They may respond to emergencies such as in domestic violence reports, severe abuse or abandonment of children. They have a particularly relevant role in cases of serious child physical abuse and in most sexual abuse cases (Murphy, 1995). Their role in these cases usually involves taking statements from victims of abuse and preparing evidential reports for use in criminal proceedings (Dale *et al.*, 1986; Murphy, 1995; Tower, 1989).

The role of the police varied considerably with regard to the different children involved in our research. For some, the police were involved in taking statements from children about their disclosures of abuse, while with others they were involved in family violence reports. Children voiced different opinions about the role of the police.

An 11-year-old girl was particularly pleased to have spoken to a policewoman instead of a policeman but also felt reassured by police intervention:

> Well, I got, I was fortunate enough to speak to a woman, which was good, and it just meant that we had to go to a police station across the road from...[name of suburb]. And I was glad that we paid that price. I'm shy around men, and I guess that's understandable...it was reassuring that something was going to be done, even though it might take a long time... They gave me a teddy too. (11 year-old female)

She is fearful, however, that the abuser will deny the abuse and that she will have to go to court:

but, yeah, we've told the police and if he denies it, then I am going to have to go to court. I don't know whether the police have done anything about it yet, because the police have usually got a lot of stuff to do. So, umm, yeah, when they get down to it he'll probably be denying it, he's a real bastard. (11-year-old female)

This 11-year-old boy, who experienced severe violence from his father, found the police role difficult to understand:

And they would say, well, why is your dad leaving and all those hard questions… Yeah, they didn't know what they were doing…most of it was for custody and all that, because then Mum didn't want Dad anywhere near the house. Like he wasn't allowed ten metres near the house. (11-year-old male)

An 11-year-old girl found the experience of talking to the police somewhat daunting:

Both times in the office, one was under, umm, video camera and the other time was just on paper. The first time it wasn't as scary because we were in a sort of brightly coloured room and there were all stuffed toys around. But the next time, there was this grey room with nothing there. (11-year-old female)

This 13-year-old boy, describes his discomfort with the police interview:

I was too scared. But there was something that was really weird about what actually happened, because some coppers were interviewing me, doing an interview, but they were asking me really weird questions, like, did these, you know, how big was his penis? And that kind of shit. And you know, and they asked me to draw it, and I was young… (13-year-old male)

This young person describes her experience of making a statement to the police. She seems to feel that the police and protective services should be able to act on even brief information obtained from the child:

I think they did a pretty good job of pushing me, but if a kid doesn't want to talk about it they won't, and I didn't, so… But I guess as far as the police and Community Services [child protection] are concerned, why should they need to know more. I mean if they discover that, yeah, there has been one or two incidents of abuse, that should be enough. I mean, I understand that, you know, that police and all that need definite cause to sort of raise things but they don't need to know everything, like from the start do they? (18-year-old female)

It can be better

Most of the children had suggestions on how the police could improve their practice. This varied from simple suggestions such as the type of room in which children are interviewed to more serious ones around the role of the police. An 11-year-old girl was quite definite that having child-friendly rooms facilitates a child's ability to make a statement:

> Yeah, make the room a sort of happy room...umm, because I found that in the grey room there was nothing really there and just the video camera and everything and it was harder to think. This wasn't in the brightly coloured room for some reason because that was sort of a more happy sort of room, it wasn't as – I don't know how to put it... Maybe, sort of, have a couch, like, counselling with the food and everything, that kind of thing. Sort of makes you feel more relaxed, like, not like the bad guys. (11-year-old female)

This 18-year-old young person explains that the decision about whether an offender should be charged or not should not be left to a child to make; she clarifies why such decisions must be made by the authorities so that the burden of responsibility and its consequences is removed from the child:

> Well if they did that [charged her father] then it wouldn't be as bad because I wouldn't have made the decision, I wouldn't have to feel guilty about it. I wouldn't have to cop all the shit from every family member, friends or whatever. So...I mean it would still be bloody hard but, you know...I'd feel like there was an actual reason for him being in jail or whatever, because the police saw reason to take action, it wasn't just something that I'd decided to do. (18-year-old female)

A view of child protection services

The increase in reports of child abuse over the years have led to child protection taking increasing priority over child welfare (Daro, 1988). Legal responsibility is placed on courts, police and social workers to take action to ensure the protection and welfare of children where there is evidence of abuse (Jones *et al.*, 1987). The need for expertise in intervening in cases of child abuse and neglect has resulted in many countries and communities developing distinct child protection services (Goddard and Carew, 1993). The responsibility for the investigation and protection of children is placed with government bodies variously referred to as child protection departments or social services departments (Daro, 1988; Goddard, 1996; Sanders, 1999; Tower, 1989). These services are mandated to assess and investigate reports of child abuse and neglect, and to invoke the authority of the courts to secure the protection, care and treatment of children (Goddard, 1996; Tower, 1989). The social worker with statutory powers plays a central role in the investigation of child abuse and protection of the child.

These child protection workers work against immense odds. They have little time in which to conduct an investigation and decide whether a child has been abused, whether he/she is safe in the home, and whether the child should be placed out of home (Corby, 1993; Goddard, 1996; Tower, 1989). Community ambivalence about the role of the state in interventions into family life creates major contradictions in child protection work. The child protection worker is left to grapple with these difficulties and uncertainties. It was therefore interesting to obtain a perspective on child protection from a young person in our research.

The protective services department was involved in three of the nine cases of the children who participated in the research. However, it was in only one case that it played a significant role, where the young person was moved into out-of-home care.

The following extracts in this section are from an 18-year-old young female who had extensive contact with child protection workers.

Introduction to child protection services

This young person describes her shock when she is told that a report has been made to child protection:

> What happened was as I sort of built up a better relationship with the school counsellor, and she started picking up on things…one day I made a bit of a slip-up and made some comment and she really pounced on that and I think it was a few days later I received a phone call from her saying that CSV [Community Services Victoria, the child protection department] had been notified…and I freaked because there was that CSV word, she said I've notified them because I'm worried about something you've said, there's going to be someone coming over to see you and that's the first I knew of it… And then I received a call from one of the workers at CSV and they arranged a meeting and told me not to tell anyone about it, but I was just freaking out.

What they did

The urgency of the protective services' role and their actions is aptly illustrated in the following extract:

> But again, I don't feel they explained things to me as well as they could have done. Well, I mean they may have done, I don't know, it was a pretty hectic time for me and I don't have crystal-clear recollections of it, but I recall my first meeting with them was up at school and they came up and they wanted me to sign a voluntary thing for them, a voluntary placement or whatever you call it, and that's the first time I'd sort of come in contact with them, and here I was faced with this yellow form and a pen and they, I kind of felt like they rushed, they just wanted to get me out of there, and then they'd look into it. Rather than sort of... I understand they can't always do that [give you more time], that there is an urgency to get the kids out of the way, but you just feel like, up in the air.

Being moved out of home

The confusion about being moved out from an abusive home to safety is succinctly described:

> It was scary but I'm in two minds about it, I mean in my mind it's the best thing that happened because I was sort of taken out of the situation from Dad and all of that. Er, it just kind of threw me into a completely different world, a completely new world. I liked the house parents at the time and built up a pretty close friendship with them, they were just amazing people. I think if they hadn't have been there I would have been crawling up the walls I think…yeah. They were fantastic…I guess you could call them substitute parents at the time and they gave so much love and attention, just great.

They were pretty terrific

Despite the frightening reality of major changes to a child's life, the type of worker and their response to the child appears to be very significant, as demonstrated in this excerpt:

> Oh, they made a huge impact… It was a pretty freaky time and really horrible at the time, but I'd have to say they were pretty fantastic. I think because of the fact that I had a brilliant worker, and it was just great to have someone with my sort of well-being in mind. I think two ladies that came out to me, whatever you call them. Yeah. They were nice too. When

I look back I'm amazed because I didn't really give them anything to go on, I only gave them, you know, I didn't sort of reveal much to them at all about what Dad did. But, umm, they kept pursuing it and you know, they took me out of my home and put me somewhere safe, so I think it was pretty amazing.

Being abandoned

The description of the sudden withdrawal of protective service involvement seems almost like another form of abuse:

But I think that they sort of left my life as quickly as they came into it. I find that really hard. They sort of come in for four or five months and turn your world upside down, pretty much, and you come to rely on them and then you're sort of told they won't be sort of involved any more and that's it. You never sort of hear from them again. Which I suppose in a way is good, because you know you've got to get on with things but I think it would really, in my case it would have been great to have maybe one or two follow-up sessions just to see how things are going and whatever.

Creating helplessness

The following comments demonstrate insight into the complexity of protective service interventions, an issue that professionals need to consider:

Yeah, the other thing about them…is the fact that they take control of your life, they run and make all the decisions for you and all that, and actually who you can and can't see, when you can and all that kind of thing. At the time that was great because, you know, Mum and Dad heaped all the shit onto them, not onto me which was fantastic, but I really found that since having them involved, I've kind of lost the ability to stand up for myself, make decisions for myself and sort of stick by those, because I'm so used to having them made for me, but now I have to make the decisions and cop whatever comes with that.

The above quotations seem to substantiate the complexity and difficulties within the child protection system, especially for child protection workers. There is a call now for a range of interventions to remedy the situation (Jones and Ramchandani, 1999; Saunders and Goddard, 1998).

Views on counselling services

As information on the impact of abuse has become more available, the need for children who have been abused to receive treatment has gained greater recognition. Working with children and families where abuse has occurred recognizes that a multi-faceted treatment approach that includes individual and family treatment, as well as a wide range of community services, is required (Wiehe, 1996). Treatment for abused children is now regarded as essential as they 'need help to sort out what has happened to them, who they are as a result of it, and to recognise all that they still can be' (MacFarlane *et al.*, 1990, p.151). Children who have been abused need to be released from the misconceptions, false learning and negative emotions that accompany abuse as they imprison children in 'a world of fear, mistrust, self-denigration and isolation long after the abuse itself has stopped' (Doyle, 1997a, p.32). Briere draws attention to the importance of individual treatment for abuse survivors: 'Abuse-focused therapy suggests that the client is not mentally ill or suffering from a defect, but rather is an individual whose life has been shaped, in part, by ongoing adaptation to a toxic environment' (1992, p.82).

Thus the goal of therapy is not recovery but the continued growth and development needed for the victim to move beyond the current level of adaptive functioning (Briere, 1992). Jones and Ramchandani (1999) state that those adults who had had access to individual, abuse-focused treatment that assisted them to cognitively process the traumatic event and make sense of it, had better outcomes and were able to achieve a more balanced appreciation of their childhood experiences.

The following section presents how children experienced the therapeutic interventions at the Centre for Children from where the sample was recruited. The Centre for Children is a specialist therapy centre for children and young people who have experienced abuse and/or family violence. The child-centred philosophy of the therapeutic programmes provided by the Centre believes in the capacity and rights of children (see Chapter 3). Children's needs and welfare are the primary concern and focus of practice. A range of innovative, child-centred therapeutic interventions, which include individual counselling, group programmes, parent/carer support and family therapy, are offered (Australians Against Child Abuse, 2001; Australian Childhood Foundation, 2003).

What I got out of counselling

Most of the children were able to verbalize the benefits of counselling. They seemed to understand that there was a more deep-seated purpose to counselling than just to help them feel good.

I'M BETTER NOW

Some children acknowledged how they had changed and in particular were able to recognize the connection between counselling and a reduction in some of their problematic behaviours, as demonstrated in the following extracts:

> Umm and then when I had counselling, like, it all changed. I was still getting into trouble but not as much and, like, I knew it wasn't my fault. I thought it was mine, but then now I know it's not mine... Umm, I learnt how to cool myself out. If I'm, like, really stressed out when people tease me, just ignore them. (12-year-old male)

> That's what I'm doing with A [counsellor] as well, because I lose my temper a lot too and that's what I'm doing. That's why I'm here because I'm seeing other ways to control my temper and that. (12-year-old female)

> Basically...like, being able to talk to someone and just that, [it's] just helpful I guess. (11-year-old female)

COUNSELLING IS EFFECTIVE

Several children were able to state that counselling had helped them let go of their anxieties and deal with their emotions:

> I think it's great. It's not fun exactly [laughs], but I don't know what to say, I mean I remember being one to sort of never talk about what's going on in my life. I've always sort of bottled things up to such an extent that if I wasn't going to counselling it would still be inside and who knows, I could well turn out to be a headcase as everyone used to make me out to be. So... (18-year-old female)

> Counselling has helped me, umm, to express my feelings, and that's why I'm not scared or anything. It improved, well...helped me understand a lot more things and stuff like that. It's really fantastic. (11-year-old female)

Another 13-year-old boy gives a more detailed account of how he feels counselling helped him:

> Umm, yeah umm, I enjoyed counselling and it has helped me, and me and my mum are having a good life now, and I am going, I have been accepted in a high school and people might reckon I am funny, but I am 13 years old and I still play with toys, but for me that is my way of calming down, because umm, toys can't get you into trouble, and toys can't give you drugs or toys can't make you do anything bad. (13-year-old male)

WHAT I LIKED BEST ABOUT COUNSELLING

The comments here convey how children felt they were helped to address the trauma of the abuse:

> What was the best part about coming to the Centre? Umm, probably how it was put into a perspective, how it was really easy to understand and, umm, and the games. That was something I looked forward to. (11-year-old female)

> It's good, like, to have fun while you're explaining it, really. Because, like, if you just explain it just sitting there it's really hard saying it. We did pieces like paper, like, I think it was gluing. Sometimes I coloured in stuff, played games. I did these sheets where you had to, umm, yeah, talk about my feelings and stuff like that really. (12-year-old male)

> Choccies, yeh [laughs]. That's good. It doesn't make it so, by the book, you know, like okay I'm here to talk. I've got to do this, that and the other. It makes it more relaxed I think, yeah. I think that's pretty important because, like I said, you guys were a big support system for me and I didn't want to come here, even though this is what the purpose is, to come here and just talk about things... Yeah. Because there were times when I just didn't want to talk about anything. But I wanted to be here because I felt safer and cared for and all that kind of thing. (18-year-old female)

Another 11-year-old girl is thoughtful in her views about counselling:

> The best part is the help. The counselling is very, very good. Well, it was really comforting because I can draw or play games and stuff like that, and...I think that kids, they can do stuff here and people don't say, now stop doing that and listen, so they can be relaxed and do what they want to, how they want to. (11-year-old female)

THE HARDEST PART ABOUT COUNSELLING

It is interesting to note that while most of the children felt they were helped to overcome the trauma of the abuse by talking about it, they also acknowledged that this was the hardest part.

This 13-year-old boy found the focus on the abuse at the beginning of counselling very hard:

> Sometimes it was boring and sometimes it was not too bad, okay. Umm, probably the worst part about counselling, umm, like, it was they wanted to know immediately what happened sort of. What happened? I didn't really feel comfortable at the start and then after a while, did I tell them? I think I did, yeah, I'm pretty sure. (13-year-old male)

A 12-year-old girl expressed a different view:

> Um, there wasn't a worst part, well, probably when I cried that would have to be the worst part. (12-year-old female)

WHAT I THOUGHT ABOUT THE COUNSELLORS

The research explored some of the children's views on the counsellors. This 13-year-old boy had developed a strong relationship with his counsellor who resigned from the Counselling Centre just prior to him finishing therapy. He is wistful about her leaving:

> M [counsellor] helped me with all my stuff, and that. Yep. She has helped me with all the problems that have gone through my life, and umm, she has helped me get my life together, because thanks to her you know, I owe her one…I don't know why she had to leave. I know she left, but, it was sad, but I still don't get it, you know, you know, probably she just wanted to get a different job, she probably got sick of what she was doing. (13-year-old male)

It can be better

Not surprisingly, many children had suggestions on how the Centre could improve its services to children. These suggestions ranged from making the counselling more fun to some ideas on extending the services – for example, involving children's support networks more closely as part of the counselling.

A BIT MORE PLAYING

An 11-year-old boy suggested that:

> Just, like, you just have a break sometimes. Ah, like, cut it down to half an hour or something and just play the games, and, talk for about 20 minutes and that's the way to do it. (11-year-old male)

This 18-year-old, as an older teenager, talks about the complexity of finding a balance when using activities in therapeutic interventions with teenagers:

> Yeah. I think you need bits and pieces, it can sort of get a bit much if you're just sitting around all the time talking and talking, whatever. Like, sometimes it was great because I just wanted to feel like a kid and be treated like a kid and it was a relief or whatever. It was good to be sort of talking about things with you guys other than the abuse. But other times it had me really shitty 'cos I didn't want to have anything to do and I was thinking, you know, I'm 17 or whatever and here I am playing games. I know it's hard, but you really need to find a balance because like I said, sometimes I just longed to feel like a kid and be treated that way, but other times, I felt years beyond my age and I just wanted to be treated like an adult and whatever. (18-year-old female)

INVOLVING CHILDREN'S SUPPORT NETWORKS

This 18-year-old also explains why she feels this should be a part of the counselling process:

> I really feel that you should work a lot more on building support systems, friends, family and all that kind of thing. Because in my case it was basically I had counselling as my support and that was all. There was nothing else there. (18-year-old female)

Message to other children about counselling

The research explored responses to the question 'So, if you were to make any suggestions to other children about counselling, what would you tell them?' The following were some of the responses that encapsulate children's views about receiving counselling for abuse:

> Well, I would tell them, you're a bit scared at the start and that, and then after a few lessons you get to know the people well, and then you'll like it, sort of. But if you keep, like, if you live the attitude like the way it is now, you won't get, like, anywhere... It's like their decision if they want

to get counselling; if they don't…well, they're really missing out; it's good really. Counselling is good. (12-year-old male)

Ah, I think they should tell those problems to the counsellor, it helps a lot. Like I said, one thing, if you've got problems go to the counsellor. They help you. (11-year-old male)

If they haven't been to a counsellor and they are still having the same problems, don't give up, just tell somebody and then it will stop. Umm, for kids who are already in counselling, probably it will help you so don't think that it's not going to and really, it's just, concentrate, because whatever the counsellor is saying it does have a meaning and you will learn something from it. (11-year-old female)

CHAPTER 9

Children as Hostages to Abuse

You've been brought up to love your parents no matter what. I don't think that I had a choice. I didn't feel like I did.

18-year-old female

Introduction

Some of the common themes that emerged from talking with children who have been abused were their helplessness to stop the abuse; their confusion about their co-existing feelings of love for the parent/family member who abused them and anger at the abuse; the feeling of being trapped in their families, and having to find ways to accommodate the abuse into their lives. Being abused in one's own home is what Forward refers to as the 'private holocaust – there's no escape' (1989, p.121). Children are helpless to move away from or avoid the abuse and are not able to protect themselves. They become hostages in their own homes, bound by the relationship between themselves and their familial abusers, and society's trust in the responsibility of parents to nurture and care for their children. This has resulted in victims of abuse having to hide their experiences of abuse (Gordon, 1990, p.xv). To tell about the abuse 'would be to betray the family' (Doyle, 1997a, p.103).

The link between the experiences of child abuse victims and those of hostages has begun to gain attention from researchers and experts in the two fields (Doyle, 1990, 1997a, 1997b; Goddard, 1988; Jones *et al.*, 1987; Wilson, 2000). Fillmore (1981, cited in Jones *et al.*, 1987) was the first to equate the frightening reality experienced by many abused children with that of a hostage or concentration camp inmate. She states, 'neither the abused child nor the camp inmate have time-limited sentences – there seems to be no end to their situation' (p.261). There are a number of features that appear to be common between hostage-taking and child abuse situations.

The value of this comparison, according to Stanley and Goddard (1995), is that it provides a framework for developing greater insights into the experiences of victimization from the child's perspective.

In this chapter we explore the links between the two theories. Drawing on the literature on political terrorism and child abuse, we summarize some of the connections between the hostage and child abuse theories. We then use the analogy to the hostage theory to present the experiences of two young people who described their abusive experiences at great length.

Summary of common links between hostage-taking and child abuse theories

We note many common features between the two theories. These include common themes in definition, personality characteristics of abusers and hostage-takers, purposes of these acts, responses by child abuse victims and hostages, and common methods used by abusers and hostage-takers. These features are summarized below.

Similarities in definition

In both child abuse and hostage-taking, violence, force and fear are the main defining characteristics. Terroristic activity is defined as 'coercive intimidation, or as the systematic use of murder, injury and destruction, or threat of same, to create a climate of terror' (Wilkinson, 1987, p.453). The violence or threat of violence is used to evoke a state of fear (or terror) in the hostage so that allegiance or compliance is maintained (Crelinsten, 1987, p.6). Child abuse includes violent acts using 'physical force so as to cause injury or forcibly interfere with personal freedom' and passive abuse that, although not considered violent, can cause physical and emotional injury (Browne, 1995, p.43). Terrorizing is one form of psychological maltreatment of children whereby an adult verbally assaults the child, bullies or frightens the child, creates a climate of fear, and makes threats of sinister punishment or threatens their daily security (Garbarino, Guttman and Seeley, 1986). From these definitions it is clear that the use of violence or threat of violence is the vehicle through which victims of terrorism and child abuse are controlled and manipulated.

Common characteristics of terrorist and abuser

Similar characteristics between abusers and terrorists include a history of impoverished social relationships, being socially isolated, a history of childhood damage, and low frustration levels (Browne, 1995; Factor and Wolfe, 1990; Post, 1990; Vondra, 1990). Wilson and Smith (2000, pp. 129–30) state that some authors explain terrorism as arising from their social backgrounds formative experiences, personality, pschodynamics and general psychiatric status.

Child abuse is explained by psychological theories (Ammerman and Hersen, 1990; Belsky, 1978; Browne, 1995; Corby, 1993), social psychological theories (Ammerman and Hersen, 1990; Browne, 1995; Corby, 1993; Gelles, 1993; Goddard, 1996) and the sociological perspectives (Ammerman and Hersen, 1990; Browne, 1995; Corby, 1993; Goddard and Carew, 1993), which show remarkable similarities to the theories on hostage-takers.

Additionally, some of the concepts, such as motivation and planning, that are explored by Wilson and Smith (2000) to understand terrorist hostage-taking can also be applied to child abuse situations. These behaviours are observed in the child abuser's ability to avoid detection, confidence in carrying out the abuse, and his/her control over others in the child's life (within and outside the home), which makes the abuser as powerful as a terrorist.

Common purpose of hostage-taking and abuse

Indiscrimination, unpredictability and destructiveness are common features of both abuse and terrorism. The most compelling behaviour of a terrorist is his/her control over a hostage, a characteristic shared with an abuser. This includes internal event control (i.e. handling of the hostages as well as all their actions and behaviours) and external control or control over external parties who may be involved – for example, those who negotiate for the hostage's release (Wilson and Smith, 2000). The extensive control over a child by an abuser renders the child submissive and co-operative. This may explain why a child who is being abused may not move away from an abusive relationship and is unable to utilize opportunities for escape (Doyle, 1990; Hatcher, 1987).

Common responses by hostages and child abuse victims

Hostages and child abuse victims demonstrate a range of common responses. Frozen fright or frozen watchfulness is one such response. This results from a paralysis of affect (Symonds, 1982) to the overwhelming unpredictability of danger and fear, likelihood of being harmed at any time and to extreme forms of deprivation, which are common responses of victims of terrorism and abuse (Corby, 1993; Hanks and Stratton, 1995). For hostages and child abuse victims, resolution of the traumatic event involves integrating the experience that may result in the development of a different sense of self. Identifying with and developing a positive bond with the hostage-taker, also referred to as Stockholm Syndrome, is a common response from hostages who have been held captive. The process develops out of a sense of guilt and can occur in either short or long periods of captivity depending on each situation (Flynn, 1987; Miller, 1980; Strenz, 1982; Symonds, 1982; Wardlaw, 1982). Similarly, children trapped in abusive situations may identify with the abuser as a way of gaining power and control to alleviate their feelings of helplessness, or they may take on some of the characteristics of the abuser as part of role modelling, which is a natural part of child development (Daro, 1988).

Common methods of the terrorist and abuser

The literature on terrorism and child abuse shows a range of similarities in methods utilized by terrorists and abusers to gain control over their victims. These include:

- the use of fear or terror to obtain compliance (Crayton,1983; Kenward and Hevey, 1992; Stanley and Goddard, 1995; Wardlaw, 1989)

- the use of power and control (Crayton, 1983; Doyle, 1997b; Gelles, 1993; Harmon, 2000; Soskis and Ochberg, 1982)

- the creation of an isolating and hostile environment (Soskis and Ochberg, 1982; Stanley and Goddard, 1995)

- dehumanizing of the victim (Bandura, 1990; Flynn, 1987; Stanley and Goddard, 1995; Wardlaw, 1989).

While there are many similarities between the two theories, there are also several features that limit the application of the terrorism and hostage theories to child abuse. However, before looking at the limitations of this relationship, we will present the connections between the hostage and child abuse theories in the context of the abusive experiences of two young people. The extensive comments made by them in our research interviews made it possible to examine their experiences within the perspectives of the hostage theory. It was also feasible to parallel their abusive encounters with current literature on terrorism and the hostage theories. How the vulnerability of children within their families predisposes them to become and remain hostages is explored. The limitations to applying this comparison are described and discussed thereafter.

Children as hostages: two young people's accounts of abuse

The names of the two young people in this section are pseudonyms chosen by them.

Eliza's story: hostage to family love and loyalty

Eliza, an 18-year-old young woman at the time of participating in the research interview, was physically and sexually abused by her father from a very early age. She also witnessed violence to her mother. She cannot remember how old she might have been when it began. For her, the abuse was as much a part of her life as 'washing the dishes or taking the dog for a walk'. She thought it was normal, and had no idea that there were words for what her father was doing to her, child abuse:

> Things were very normal for me. I saw things as being very normal. I didn't know any differently. I didn't think there was a problem.

Eliza also believed that her family was ordinary and normal:

> They seemed so normal and that really put doubts in my mind about the abuse and everything. You know, I've got a mum who's got a full-time job and you know, has lots of friends and goes out and does things on the weekends, and a dad who sits at a desk all day and goes running in the mornings and whatever, and everyone loves him and he's got a great sense of humour and…it sounds pretty normal to me.

With such a background, Eliza thought all was fine in her life. Her family was financially secure and she wanted for nothing. She was very close to her mother and enjoyed her relationship with her father:

> Yeah, we had a pretty good relationship, we had a lot of good times together.

Yet she knew something was not right, she felt different from other children but she found it difficult to know what was wrong in her life:

> I always sort of knew when I was a little tacker in primary school that, that I was just basically different to the rest of my friends. I just felt years ahead of them… And it was a real issue at times. So things were pretty difficult.

With the abuse firmly ingrained into the fabric of her life, Eliza learned to accommodate it into her life. When children are powerless to stop the abuse, acceptance of the abuse becomes a means of survival (Cashmore and Bussey, 1988). Eliza became a victim. When she was six, she was sexually abused on several occasions by an adult male friend of the family who was allegedly having an affair with her mother. When she was ten or eleven years old, she was sexually abused by several teenage boys who were friends of her older brother.

It was around this time, because of her academic problems that:

> they [Eliza's parents] sent me along to the school counsellor and things sort of slowly over the years unravelled and that's when I sort of started thinking more that things maybe aren't quite normal

But her attempts to find out what was wrong proved fruitless:

> Um, there weren't a lot of options really. I mean there were a lot of times I sort of tried talking to Mum about it and umm, all sorts of strategies to use at home. I often used to get books out of the library on abuse and whatever, to see if what was happening to me was valid or whether it was real or, you know. If it was in a book it must be real, but half the stuff that happened to me, or my situation, weren't in the damn books. So I was thinking, oh shit, something's wrong here, it must be in my head…you read all these textbooks about abuse and you see all these things on the news and…and the abuser is some alcoholic…and the mother's a psycho, and living in the slums and whatever, it always confused the heck out of me because I think hang on, my family's not like that, you know. They seem so normal and that really put doubts in my mind about the abuse and everything.

By the age of 13, Eliza found she had nowhere to go and no one she could go to for help who could explain to her what was going on in her life. She felt trapped and silenced. She had become a hostage to the abuse and to her father who, like a terrorist, had caused her to become compliant and powerless (Bandura, 1990). Eliza did not disclose the abuse to anyone nor did she need to be told not to tell. Summit (1983) explains why a child may not tell. Abuse happens when the child is alone with the adult and the child gradually learns that this is something that is not shared with anyone else. 'The average child never asks and never tells' (p.181). In fact, if the child is young and there is an established relationship of affection and authority, there is little risk of discovery as 'Dependent children are helpless to resist or complain' (p.183). Additionally, role reversal, a significant feature in child abuse, gives the power to the child to destroy or keep the family intact (Summit, 1983). Eliza says, 'You know, I mean, despite what Dad's done to me I didn't want to sort of tear up the whole family.'

The emotional confusion for the child is then shown in 'psychological disorganisation' (Howe, 1996, p.13), which results in contradictory attachment behaviours. Eliza's relationship with her father is confusing for her. Rather than an absence of attachment or insecure attachment, Stanley and Goddard (1995) suggest that there are features of disturbed or pathological attachment. Eliza describes the dysfunctional attachment between her and her father:

> I know he does love me...if you compare it to now, it was great. There was no tension between the two of us, there was no, sort of none of the bullshit that goes on now.

Cashmore and Bussey (1988) state that physical demonstrations of affection by an adult, especially a parent to a child happens spontaneously – for example, hugging a child, ruffling their hair or patting them. Children may therefore find it difficult to 'distinguish between such "affectionate" behaviour and sexually exploitative behaviour' (p.15). In hostage and abuse situations, basic human needs such as the need to belong, and for love and esteem are violated (Soskis and Ochberg, 1982). The psychological isolation that accompanies most forms of abuse, and especially sexual abuse, interferes most with the need for a sense of belonging and love. Eliza again:

> but the way I see it...I mean for starters they're my parents, the only parents I've got, and as warped as their love may be, they still love me and that's like the most important thing to me, is to have people who love me and care for me... So it's a hard thing to give up.

Eliza's experience as a hostage to the disturbed attachments within her family is poignantly clear in the following statement:

> You've been brought up to love your parents no matter what. I don't think that I had a choice. I didn't feel like I did…I didn't tell many people before I left home, but yeah, the few people that I did would say 'Get out, do something about it.' But I was only what?…15 or something, I wasn't an adult. You're not exactly equipped with the emotional or mental stuff to do that. And in a lot of cases, the thing that people don't understand is that yes, your dad may abuse you or your mother or whatever, but you still love them, you still have feelings for them, they're still your parents and you don't want to lose them.

Being trapped emotionally by the abuser's power results in the child's inability to utilize opportunities for escape (Doyle, 1990; Hatcher, 1987). Stanley and Goddard (1995) suggest that the hostage theory provides a framework for understanding the child's reality, the confusion and ambivalence that a child in this situation experiences, and the inability to move out of the abusive relationship. As Eliza says:

> but what really used to get to me is people would ask well, 'Why are you still home, why don't you get out and get some help' and 'It's easy' and all this kind of thing. There's nothing worse than someone saying, get out when they just have no idea 'cos it's just kind of like, you feel stuck there. And you're used to it, and in my case it was what I knew, it was my life, it was just, you know… And to get out of it was to face the unknown. You don't know what's on the other side and you don't know if it's going to be better or worse or what. So, you know, it's kind of like a disease, it's pretty hard to break free, so…

Eliza found various ways to cope with the confusion of her life:

> Yeah, I have a habit of blocking things out. I think I'm an expert at that. … Sort of maybe it was born in me…[I also] turned to ways of denying all the pain and the issues and whatever. I went through a stage with drinking and the drugs and that didn't particularly help. I was a great one for the old self-mutilation as well.
>
> I think what happens with most kids, is they grow up so quick, I had to grow up too quickly and I just feel like I missed out on childhood pretty much. Which is a pretty huge thing to cope with. Yeah, at times I still feel like I'm sort of stuck there, back in childhood. I didn't really have a choice, you have to grow up pretty fast in that sort of situation, otherwise you don't survive. It's as simple as that.

In the course of seeing the school counsellor, Eliza eventually began to divulge the abuse she experienced by the family friend and the teenage boys. It was during this time that she inadvertently disclosed some aspects of the sexualized relationship with her father that led to protective service involvement and exposure of the family secret. Eliza's view of this intervention and its impact on her relationship with her father reflects the dysfunctional attachment she has with him. She mourns the loss of that 'comfortable', abusive relationship she had with him previously, noting that with disclosure and intervention 'It's screwed things up completely.'

Scorpion's story: hostage to family violence

Scorpion, a 13-year-old young person, was nearly four years old when the abuse began and, in his words, 'my life went bad and you know, this S [abuser], this mean devil used to be nasty to me all the time'.

Scorpion goes on to describe how his life went bad:

> Um, well, [he] used to bash my mum up, and you know, like you see your mum get bashed up and you almost got killed once, and you know, so you know, you are not a normal, you wouldn't be a normal person if you are going through something like that. I used to think he was an animal, but a bloody animal wouldn't even do that, an animal don't bash their own up.

Scorpion was also regularly beaten, threatened with cigarette burns and punished by being made to sit naked in a corner for many hours. These physically violent and psychologically terrorizing acts of abuse (Browne, 1995; Garbarino et al., 1986) are similar to actions described in the literature on hostage-taking, which suggests that there is 'the deliberate creation of fear for coercive purposes' (Flynn, 1987, p.337) that is used to evoke allegiance or compliance in a particular victim (Crelinsten, 1987). It is apparent from Scorpion's description that his abusive experiences closely resemble the experiences of a hostage. Goddard and Hiller (1993a) say that the state of fear or terror can be exacerbated for the child abuse victim by the use of violence against others – in Scorpion's case, the violence against his mother. 'Children having witnessed the beating of their mothers need no further reminder of the possible consequences of their resistance to the wishes of their fathers (or, indeed, of older males in general)' (Goddard and Hiller, 1993a, p.27).

Scorpion's terror is transparent in the following extract:

> he said he was going to blow us away…and I'm tellin' yer, I did shit my pants. I thought about if I would survive, and in the end, would Mum live.

The most notable behaviour of a terrorist and abuser is his/her control over the hostage or victim. Scorpion describes the abuser's control over his mother through violence and persuasion, which made Scorpion feel totally unprotected and helpless:

> Because he threatened my mum, but see, Mum was too scared to do anything, because he would, like she didn't know what he was doing to me, until she started…she started to get bashed up, but you know, she got sucked in, you know what men are like… I felt like I was let down with Mum, because, like she…you know, like she let herself get sucked in three times.

'Children who are subject to a chronic pattern of serious physical abuse and neglect live in a very unpredictable world' (Kenward and Hevey, 1992, p.206). The abuser uses violence or threats of unpredictable and impending violence to ensure compliance from the child (Goddard and Stanley, 1994). The increased violence, sexual abuse and ritual abuse that this child was further subjected to sealed his terror and therefore his compliance. There was no escape from this life of terror for Scorpion. At the tender age of five or six, this child tried to work out what to do to protect himself and to fight back:

> [I used to think] how the f— am I going to get out of this? …actually, I kicked him in the head once; and I tried to get the keys, but I couldn't because he was down on the ground, and then he woke up and boy oh boy, didn't I get it.

Children cannot protect themselves and have to accept that avoiding the abuse is beyond their control (Briere, 1992). How, then, did this child survive the horror of his life? What impact did such terrifying, incomprehensible experiences have on him?

When children are trapped in abusive situations, the personality is formed and deformed by the repeated trauma and 'some children…begin to form separated personality fragments with their own names, psychological and sequestered memories' (Herman, 1992, p.102). Hostage theorists believe that victims of terrorism, in their attempt to resolve the hostage experience, have to develop new patterns of behaviour that give them control over their lives (Crayton, 1983; Flynn, 1987). The experience of the terror is so damaging to the hostage's mind and body that they 'will never be as they were before' (Flynn, 1987, p.352) and this amounts to the 'death of self' (p.342). This may mean destroying their original identity and taking on a new personality, or becoming a different person. In the child abuse literature, this is referred to as the development of multiple personality disorder. Kluft (1998) states that a child who is subject to severe trauma such as abuse may repeatedly use dissociation to deal with the extreme stress, which can lead to the creation of multiple personality disorder. Although this disorder is usually diagnosed in adulthood, 'The first dissociation almost always occurs in childhood, usually in the context of immediate, overwhelming trauma' (p.9).

For this child to survive, he created a new identity, a character from a movie and video game who is violent and powerful. He describes how the powerless and compliant Martin (name changed) has been replaced by this powerful and invincible identity:

> Hi, my name is Scorpion…he is one of the characters from *Mortal Kombat* of course…like I used to be really different when I was Martin [name changed], but like I am completely different when I am Scorpion…like I am more powerful than what I am, and I'm like an immortal now, because like, everything of me has been put back in, but I haven't got a, Martin…hasn't got a soul…and Martin's soul got destroyed and so, but I am Scorpion, I am 100 per cent Scorpion. He is me.

Commentary

This section has presented the stories of Eliza and Scorpion in the context of hostage theory (Mudaly, 1998, 2002; Mudaly and Goddard, 2001b). Children are taught to love and honour their parents and do so even when abused by them. Because of their trained obedience and vulnerability (Briere, 1992), these two young people describe how they had to accommodate the violent and sadistic behaviours by their paternal carers into their lives.

The invidious effects of long-term sexual abuse and the horror of violence to children are experiences that go beyond the developmental ability of children to comprehend. While their experiences of abuse appear on the surface to be different, the responses of Eliza and Scorpion as vulnerable and powerless children trapped in these traumatic situations demonstrate much similarity. Their circumstances, we suggest, may be equated to those of hostages of terrorism. Eliza's and Scorpion's stories tell us what some children do to survive abuse.

The similarity in experiences for child abuse and terrorist victims has already been referred to. A common experience is their 'inescapable encounter with...terrible events' (Soskis and Ochberg, 1982, p.111) which can be so overwhelming as to go beyond a child's defence mechanisms or coping strategies. The impact of terrorization on children is more significant since their ego capacity is not yet developed enough to withstand all the terrible factors associated with hostage-taking (Fields, 1982). The child may constantly be threatened with 'life-destroying violence and often receives violence for no consistent reason' (Fillmore, 1981, cited in Jones *et al.*, 1987, p.260). Scorpion says of his experience of frequent and unexpected violence and abuse that he would often be 'thinking of what I had done, what did I do wrong'. The sense of isolation, of shame and guilt as well as blame are experiences both sexual abuse victims and hostages encounter from being coerced into participation (Soskis and Ochberg, 1982; Summit, 1983). The child who is sexually abused by the father and rejected by the mother 'is psychologically orphaned and almost indefensible against multiple harmful consequences' (Summit, 1983, p.179). Eliza's experience of sexual abuse by her father and abandonment by her mother resulted in her multiple abusive experiences by several other people.

Stanley and Goddard suggest that little has been written on the long-term impact of the developmental disruptions that accompany abuse. But, they say, 'We do know from the terrorist literature, that the experience of being a hostage may be so dominating even for a mature adult, that it has the effect of dis-engaging the person from other relationships and society in general' (1995, p.27).

Eliza, trapped in a situation from which she had no way out, had withdrawn into silence:

> I remember being one to sort of never talk about what's going on in my life. I've always sort of bottled things up to such an extent that if I wasn't going to counselling, it would still be inside and who knows, I could well turn out to be a headcase as everyone used to make me out to be.

Scorpion's disengagement from society and from reality is more pronounced and dramatic. He chose to dissociate from the powerless child and take on the identity of a powerful fantasy character:

> Martin [name changed] is dead, because he got destroyed, and Martin's soul got destroyed and so, but I am Scorpion. He is a part of me and my life because, umm, he is in me and like in a way he is me, you know.

There is value in drawing attention to the similarity in the experiences of child abuse victims and those of political hostages. It can give a valuable insight into and understanding of some of the behaviours displayed by children who are abused, as in Scorpion's story (Mudaly, 2001; Mudaly and Goddard, 2001b; Stanley and Goddard, 1995). It can also provide insights into the strength and impact of the abusive relationship on the child's development, as noted in the experience of Eliza. The psychological impact of being a hostage, for the 'young child who has never had the opportunity to establish basic trust, ego identity, and object permanency and consistency must be addressed or the effect can damage the child's life and future generations' (Goddard and Stanley, 1994, p.266).

Limitations of the application of hostage theory to child abuse

While the comparison with hostage theory shows many similarities, some of the experiences of child abuse victims appear to be vastly different.

Publicity versus secrecy

Terrorism and hostage situations are always publicized as they are usually public acts that use publicity in order to publicize the group's or individual's cause (Harmon, 2000; Wilkinson, 1987). The hostage experience is not a secret and there is often public belief in and sympathy for the hostage's experiences. With child abuse victims, however, this is a significant difference. The abuse is a secret and the responsibility for disclosing it and stopping the abuse is devolved onto the child (Cashmore and Bussey, 1988). This places the child in a very difficult position whereby the child's disclosure can result in the break-up of the family. Eliza clearly describes her dilemma when she says 'despite what Dad's done to me I didn't want to sort of tear up the whole family' nor did she want her father to go to jail. Eliza therefore had to find a way to preserve her relationship with her father in spite of the abuse. Herman states that the child will do this 'even at the sacrifice of their own welfare, their own reality, or their lives' (1992, p. 98). For Eliza this meant being branded a 'headcase' by her family.

Threats of violence versus absence of threats

Another limitation of applying hostage theory to child abuse situations is that it does not explain that some abusers do not have to use threats of violence or brutality to gain compliance and submission in their victims. While Scorpion's abuser seems to fit the general description of the terrorist, this is not the case with Eliza's father. He was the source of affection and attention as well as abuse. He appears to have led her to believe that the abuse was a demonstration of his deep love for her. Cashmore and Bussey explain that some forms of sexual contact may provide 'a positive and pleasurable experience for the child, since someone is paying attention and being affectionate towards them' (1988, p.14). Eliza describes her strong belief in her father's love for her:

> I know he [father] does love me, I know he loves me a heck of a lot, and I always just figured it was just over-fondness or something.

Choosing a hostage versus children who are targets of abuse

A further issue that differentiates these two theories is that of how hostages and victims of abuse are chosen. The targets of terrorism are carefully selected to promote the terrorist's best chance of achieving his/her goals (Cordes, 1987). This may also apply in certain aspects of child abuse. In sexual abuse of children, for example, a victim is chosen carefully so that the abuser is able to engage the child into secrecy and non-disclosure. Generally, however, choice of victims is not as specific in child abuse as it is in terrorism or hostage-taking situations. Finkelhor explores why this is so and states that *'Children have comparatively little choice over whom they associate with, less choice perhaps than any segment of the population besides prisoners'* (1997, p.93, Finkelhor's italics for emphasis).

He explains that children who live in abusive families are not free or able to leave, nor are they able to move away from dangerous neighbourhoods or schools where they may be bullied or harmed. They have less choice in terms of avoiding danger and abuse even when they perceive it. The following quotation from a 12-year-old research participant is testimony of this:

> That's probably because [with my dad] I was the closest one and probably the same thing with my grandfather, because I was the easiest target. It's like, it would be too difficult to go out into a shopping centre or something and catch whoever comes into the toilet or something and I was there at the time. (12-year-old girl)

Relationship between captor and hostage versus abuser and child victim

The terrorist is usually a stranger to the hostage, which together with the suddenness and unpredictability of the act, make it extremely frightening (Wardlaw, 1989). In contrast, abuse of children often happens by persons known to the child and who have the responsibility for the care and nurture of the child (Angus and Wilkinson, 1993; Doyle, 1997a; Gil, 1975; Goddard, 1996). There is usually an established relationship between the child and the abuser(s). Stanley and Goddard state that 'Instead of a secure, nurturing person for the child to turn to when experiencing anxiety or fear, the caregiver him or herself may be an additional source of fear' (1995, p.26).

This can be extremely confusing for children given their cognitive limitations to understand the dynamics of abuse. In some forms of abuse – for example, sexual abuse – the abuser deliberately misleads the child into believing that the abuse is a demonstration of his/her profound love for the child. Cashmore and Bussey state that 'adults, and parents in particular…assume immense importance in the eyes of children' and children will therefore naturally 'comply with the wishes of a sexually abusive adult family member' (1988, p.15). Abuse within their own homes traps children in a situation from which there is no escape (Doyle, 1997b). Children's dependence on their parents leads them to adapt to the abuse within the home in a way that preserves the relationship with the parents in spite of the abuse (Herman, 1992). 'This is the most powerful way in which the child's voice is silenced' (Atwool, 2000, p.21).

Conclusion

The comparison between the child abuse and hostage literature draws attention to the following specific issues for abused children.

- Children's dependence on adults for their care: 'the young child is wholly dependent for his welfare and for life itself on the care bestowed on him by grown-ups' (Bowlby, 1967, p.148). In abusive situations, the abusive parent may actually be the 'source of pain, fear and denigration to the child' (Stanley and Goddard, 1995, p.27). This places children in a helpless and frightening situation as the way in which society is organized to rear children is within the privacy of the family (Parton, 1990). Children become trapped in this abusive environment and relationship where they are 'most frequently manipulated, coerced, degraded, inoculated with destructive beliefs and exposed to violence' (Perry, 2000, p.3). While the plight of children who are abused within their families may be equated to that of hostages of terrorism, the secrecy that surrounds abuse and children's developmental dependence on the abusing adult, makes child abuse a more alarming crime and intervention more difficult.

- Children entrapped in such circumstances have to find ways to accommodate this paradoxical situation. The child and political hostage may accommodate in a similar way by establishing a disturbed attachment with the abuser characterized by 'fear or wariness of their attachment figure…and contradictory attachment behaviours' (Cicchetti, 1987, cited in Stanley and Goddard, 1995, p.27). This relationship therefore distorts the child's ability to relate to and interact with other adults and peers in their current and future lives. It impedes the development of self-esteem, social skills, problem solving and independence from parents (Peterson, 1996).

- While such an attachment helps a child survive abusive experiences, the costs to the child's development are serious. Stanley and Goddard (1995) cite many child development specialists and draw attention to the child's inability to successfully complete the stages in their development. The impact on the child will naturally be greater than adult experiences of being a hostage.

Stanley and Goddard (1995) suggest that this comparison can further the understanding and responses to children who are abused. In particular, the type of therapy that these children require is an issue that needs further work. This would enable professionals to make more meaningful contributions to helping children who are abused overcome the long-term impact of their experiences (Mudaly and Goddard, 2001a). The need for skilled therapy for child hostages has been called for, as the hostage experience for children leaves deep scars at the emotional level. These have 'important ramifications for attempts of interventions designed to provide counselling and psychotherapy' (Desivilya, Gal and Ayalon, 1996, p.148). Children who are abused are at high risk of developing abusive patterns of behaviour (Bentovim, 2002). Careful thought and attention therefore needs to be given to the importance of modifying treatment approaches to intervene into the potential long-term, pervasive impact of abuse.

The comparison between the hostage theories and child abuse is in its early stages, and the studies by Stanley and Goddard (1993a, 1993b, 1995, 2002) and Goddard and Stanley (1994) appear to be pioneering ones in this regard. Many aspects of the comparison would benefit from further work. For example, it would be useful to explore whether the association with terrorism and hostage-taking, and the publicity and attention that these acts generate, would contribute to increasing public awareness of the severe effects of abuse for children.

CHAPTER 10

Children's Vulnerability to Abuse

A Double-edged Issue

...probably because they're [children] not smart enough to know what's happening, like, they're not old enough to know it's, like, wrong.

12-year-old male

Introduction

Despite society's increased awareness of child abuse and the need to protect children, the abuse of children continues to be a major social problem (Browne, 1995; Daro, 1988; Goddard, 1996; Mullens and Fleming, 1998). What makes children susceptible to abuse? In this chapter we explore this question with a particular focus on children's vulnerabilities within families and in broader society. The views expressed by children about their vulnerability to abuse are woven into the discussion throughout the chapter, demonstrating their insight on this issue and helplessness to prevent abuse.

Children's vulnerability appears to be entwined in two contradictory perceptions that adults have of children: that they are 'vulnerable' and that they are 'incompetent' (Morrow and Richards, 1996, p.96). According to King (1997), this formulation of childhood as a period of vulnerability and irresponsibility seems to set up this perverse dichotomy. In addition, conceptualizing children as dependants has led to them being 'subsumed within families and excluded' (Mayall, 1994, p.4).

Children's inherent developmental vulnerability, and their structural vulnerability according to Lansdown (1994; see also Briere, 1992; Summit, 1990), are the key issues to consider when exploring children's vulnerability to abuse. According to Briere (1992) this structural vulnerability includes certain societal and socialization factors, such as children's lesser status in society and trained obedience to parents, which contribute to children's susceptibility to abuse. These issues, children's developmental and structural vulnerabilities, are discussed in detail here.

Developmental vulnerability

All living things develop within a context. For the child, the family, culture, community, immediate surroundings and time in history provide that context (Sroufe, Cooper and DeHart, 1992). In all societies, families are expected to care for and nurture children, to provide for them financially, and to transmit cultural and moral traditions and values (Bowes and Watson, 1999). The family therefore remains the most significant primary context for the child's development. 'Family members stimulate cognitive development, model various roles and behaviours, provide nurturing relationships, and filter other developmental influences' (Sroufe *et al.*, 1992, p.75). Historically it was 'generally believed that children will be cherished and nurtured by their parents. A parent's love for his or her child is seen as part of the natural order of things...and believed to be universal' (Goddard, 1996, p.30).

Families therefore have a major impact on children's lives as the emotional intensity of families means that learning in this context is likely to be extensive and long-lasting (Bowes and Watson, 1999). But the family has changed significantly over the years to cope with the high-pressure, industrialized and impersonal world of today (Tower, 1989). Contemporary families in most countries, including Australia, now include single female or male parent families, both parents in employment, blended families or parents in de facto relationships. The family may be one where a group of people live together and share the basic tasks of daily life including taking primary responsibility for the rearing of children (Tower, 1989). These changes have implications for the place of children in the family and the meaning and roles of parenthood (Tomison, 1996). If the context is abnormal, inadequate or depriving, development is similarly affected (Sroufe *et al.*, 1992). Adults' perceptions of children as developmentally immature, together with their dependence on adults for caretaking, and society's belief in the sanctity of the family, perhaps increase children's vulnerability to abuse.

Children's developmental issues

During childhood, children are inherently vulnerable because of their small physical stature and their relative lack of experience, which increase their dependence on adults (Briere, 1992; Finkelhor, 1997; Morrow and Richards, 1996). This makes them more likely to be abused. The following quotations demonstrate children's insight into their developmental vulnerability to abuse:

> Well, they're picking on people who are smaller than them…and weaker than them. (12-year-old female)

> [T]here's this little kid who just doesn't have anything, any control over their life yet. (11-year-old female)

> [B]ecause kids are smaller and kids can't fight back when they are young. (13-year-old male)

Children's dependency

Children, especially during infancy, depend for their very survival on adults through the structure of the family (Archard, 1993). This makes children more prone to abuse because children are raised within the privacy of the family (Parton, 1990). The dependence on the adults around them also makes children easy targets and accessible to victimization. 'Children have comparatively little choice over whom they associate with' and this can put them into contact with high-risk offenders (Finkelhor, 1997, p.93).

> Well, the problem is you don't know beforehand, you don't know really what's going to happen or anything in the future. I mean, if it hadn't happened to you before or something then you just don't know…you don't really know why it is happening until you go to counselling. (11-year-old female)

Children may therefore be at risk of abuse trapped by their dependence on adults, and society's continued acceptance of the privacy of families. The privacy awarded to the family unit, 'makes child abuse less detectable and easier to commit' as there are fewer constraints on expressing emotions aggressively (Browne, 1995, p.47).

Children's helplessness

Children's developmental vulnerability also prevents them from being able to 'retaliate or deter victimisation as effectively as those with more strength and power' (Finkelhor, 1997, p.93). Finkelhor goes on to explain that vulnerable adults, such as women experiencing violence, still have more choices than children to protect themselves from danger. Children do not have the same ability as adults to move out of situations and relationships that are dangerous or hostile to them. They are therefore more vulnerable to both familial and societal victimization: 'Whatever boundaries of childhood are drawn, they are, as a group of people, comparatively more vulnerable than adults, and therefore require special measures to protect and promote their needs' (Lansdown, 1994, p.34).

Young children are particularly predisposed to abuse when it occurs in an established relationship of love and authority between child and parent (Summit, 1983). Politically, children are still mainly understood within the parent/child relationship (Mayall, 1999). The relationships between parents and children are regarded as mutually beneficial as both parents and children are rewarded by mutual expressions of love (Goddard, 1996). Therefore the impact on the child of being abused by a parent whom he or she loves can be extremely confusing:

> but the way I see it, I mean for starters they're my parents, the only parents I've got… You've been brought up to love your parents no matter what. I don't think I had a choice. I didn't feel like I did. (18-year-old female)

> [With my dad] I was the closest one and the same thing with my grandfather, I was the easiest target… It is a bit harder with Dad though, because he's my dad, and I know he did that sort of thing to me, but it's a bit harder. (11-year-old female)

Silenced by abuse

Children may become trapped in abusive situations, silenced by their ambivalent feelings towards their familial abusers. Summit (1983) states that a child does not have to be told to keep the abuse secret. They learn that abuse must not be shared with anyone else.

> You know, I mean, despite what Dad's done to me I didn't want to sort of tear up the whole family…the thing that people don't understand is that yes, your dad may abuse you or your mother or whatever, but you still

love them, you still have feelings for them, they're still your parents and you don't want to lose them. (18-year-old female)

Sometimes witnessing the violence of an abuser to others is enough to let the child know the consequences of disclosure (Goddard and Hiller, 1993a, p.27).

> my life went bad and you know, this S [name of abuser], this mean devil used to be nasty to me all the time, used to bash my mum up, and you know, you see your mum get bashed up and you almost got killed once, and you know, so you know, you are not a normal, you wouldn't be a normal person if you are going through something like that. (13-year-old male)

> [A]nd with my dad, he knew I didn't like Mum and Dad fighting because um, um, he threatened that they'd fight and that was enough to make me shut up. (11-year-old female)

Developmental vulnerability of children is an inherent part of being a child. The same qualities that make children worthy of love and care make them vulnerable to abuse (Summit, 1990). In advocating for accepting children's developmental vulnerability, Summit states, 'Children will be less vulnerable when we, as protective adults, can understand how exquisitely vulnerable they are' (p.73).

Rather than reinforce views of children's incompetence by portraying them as victims, we have to develop methods that allow us to explore children's capacities, needs and interests from their own points of view (Thomas and O'Kane, 1998, p.346). Yet, children's developmental vulnerability appears to be the basis for their lack of full social and political participation in society. This, in turn, appears to contribute to their structural vulnerability.

Structural vulnerability

Goddard (1996, p.15) states that 'while children are valued, there are limits to how much emphasis a society is prepared to place on those rights when they are in conflict with the rights and interests of others'.

Society's ambivalent attitude to children, together with the view of them as a subordinate group, have led to children having little status, no voice and no political power. They are excluded from full participation in the life of society. Children are structurally vulnerable because of their 'total lack of political and economic power and their lack of civil rights' (Lansdown, 1994, p.35). According to Franklin (1995) governments ignore children because children do not have a vote, and do not lobby decision-makers. The various factors that contribute to children's structural vulnerability are now discussed further.

The status of childhood

Although there is now a general acceptance that childhood is a normal and natural stage of development, and one that everyone must go through (Jenks, 1996), childhood has continued to be regarded as inferior to adulthood. As early as the fifteenth century, childhood was defined as a period when a person was temporarily bounded by incapacity, and seen as 'parasitic' on 'adulthood' because children lacked physical independence and the capacity to reason as adults (Locke, 1632–1704, cited in Archard, 1993, p.11). Hoyles and Evans assert that the current myth of childhood 'portrays children as not being political or sexual, as depending wholly on adults, and never engaged in serious activities such as work or culture' (1989, p.10).

One reason for this view is that, until recently, childhood was not viewed as a separate stage of human development (Goddard, 1996, p.7). The social construction model explains childhood as not having a constant, finite form but as a 'historically shifting, cultural construction' (Franklin, 1986, p.7). The point at which childhood ends, and adulthood begins, is not fixed and may occur at different ages according to different spheres of activities (Franklin, 1995). There is, for example, a voting age, a driving age, and an age old enough to be held legally liable for a crime (Archard, 1993; Goddard and Carew, 1993). Because of this elasticity and because childhood is seen as transitory, a stage we grow out of on our way to our final destination, which is adulthood, it is not accorded an equal status to that of adulthood (Jenks, 1996).

The developmental model of childhood, arising from developmental psychology, and which has a strong influence on childcare policy and practice, is also grounded in this deficit approach of conceptualizing childhood (Mullender et al., 2002). Children are defined as 'becomings' (Mason, 1999, p.28) rather than as beings. Childhood is seen as a period of 'laying down the foundations, as shaping the individual; taking on; growing up; preparation; inadequacy; inexperience; immaturity' (Jenks, 1996, p.9). It is seen as a period of incompetence in relation to adulthood, a period that does not have the capacities, skills and powers of adulthood (Archard, 1993). In fact, childhood 'has often been mythologised as the "golden age" in which children, untroubled by the adult concerns of work and economic life, are free to enjoy themselves' (Franklin, 1995, p.7). This 'adultcentric' perspective of childhood, which promotes maintenance of adult interests (Mason, 1999, p.28), has led to 'a failure to integrate childhood into society as an important and inherent part of human development' (Mayall, 1994, p.4). This view is seen as justifying welfare policies that emphasize children's value only as future adults (Mason, 1999). Children's experiences of childhood and their social contexts are ignored. Mason describes this as the invisibility of the 'present' child (p.30). Instead, the focus of professionals is on 'the universal child', on children as part of families and not as individuals in their own right. Children's welfare and protection has largely been monitored through 'surveillance of deviant families' (Mason, 1999, p.30).

Children as lesser beings

The undervaluing of childhood has consequently influenced the conceptualizations and views of children. Defining a child is no easy task (Goddard and Carew, 1993). Issues related to age, culture and the particular time in society influence how a child is defined and viewed. The flexibility in regard to where childhood ends and adulthood begins, has resulted in confusion about the term child and who can be regarded as a child. The *Concise Oxford Dictionary* defines a child as 'a young human being; a person who has not reached [an] age of discretion' (Sykes, 1983, p.160) yet the literature describes children in negative terms such as:

- 'non-adults' (Franklin, 1986, p.7)

- 'weak, vulnerable and incapable of providing for their own maintenance' (Locke, 1632–1704, cited in Archard, 1993, p.7)

- an innocent incompetent being who is not an adult but must become one (Archard, 1993).

This view of children as non-adults presents children as different to adults. The 'child is familiar to us and yet strange', which in itself is odd since to be an adult one has had to be a child first (Jenks, 1996, p.3). The child's world is seen as different (Archard, 1993; Petr, 1998). Play, a natural part of a child's world, is seen as unimportant and as the opposite of work, which only adults engage in and which society regards as all-important.

This view of children as different from and not as good as adults seems to stem from an attitude described as 'adultcentrism' (Mason, 1999; Petr, 1998). Petr defines this as 'the tendency of adults to view children and their problems from a biased, adult perspective', which is based on a belief that the adult way is right and best (Petr, 1998, p.16). The inability to appreciate children in their own right, rather than as non-adults, has led Greer (1984) to suggest that western society has developed an attitude of not liking children. Greer's controversial proposal is made in the context of exploring the place of the child in the modern world. She states that, historically, human societies were pro-child, while 'modern society is unique in that it is profoundly hostile to children...because we do not like them' (1984, p.2). She proposes that children do not fit easily into the western adult's lifestyle. Some of the reasons suggested are that children are obstacles to women achieving in their careers, are an economic drain on the family, and place pressure on relationships, causing marital breakdowns (Goddard and Carew, 1993). Greer's views, of course, are contradicted by De Mause (1974, p.1) who argues that 'the further back in history one goes, the lower the level of child care'.

The historical construction of children as either inherently good and innocent, or evil and bad, is another factor that influences attitudes to children (Franklin, 2001; James, Jenks and Prout, 1998). The idea of children as innocent, pure and joyful, and therefore society's hope for the future, promotes a need to preserve and protect these qualities and therefore to protect the child. On the other hand, the view of the child as evil promotes attitudes of constraining and punishing children (James *et al.*, 1998). The demonizing by the media of children who engage in anti-social and criminal activities (which reached a peak in Britain over the murder of James Bulger by two ten-year-old boys), also set back progress on children's rights (Franklin, 2001). It 'prompted a predictable retreat in some areas from policies intended to promote and protect children's rights' (Franklin, 1995, p.5). These binary views on children, fuelled by media campaigns on high-profile cases of young offenders, have therefore impaired any steady development of positive attitudes towards children, and to giving recognition to children as a social group with rights and privileges of their own. Franklin states that 'recent progress in achieving rights for children has been faltering and uneven' (1995, p.5).

Attitudes that see children as less than adults, as burdens, as the property of parents, as liabilities, and as threats to adults' rights and privileges are deeply ingrained in current society. These attitudes influence efforts to recognize children as a social group in their own right and to acknowledge the importance of the experiences and preoccupations specific to this stage of development.

Children's needs versus their rights

Presumptions about the nature of childhood and children have therefore rendered children and young people who are abused socially vulnerable, powerless and silenced (Edwards and Alldred, 1999). This has led to tensions in recognizing that children have rights and not just needs (Lansdown, 1994). It is important to distinguish between children's moral and legal rights and between welfare and liberty rights (Franklin, 1995). This has been the subject of much debate, which:

> exposes the inherent tension between a view of children on the one hand, as dependent on adult protection and incapable of taking responsibility for their decision-making, and on the other, as people with basic civil rights including the right to participate fully in decisions that affect their lives. (Lansdown, 1994, p.36)

Lansdown further states that the development of society's laws, policies and practice relies too heavily on children's biological and psychological vulnerability and less on how their lack of civil status creates that vulnerability. Society, according to Leach (1990), is set up to disregard and neglect children and their specific needs and rights. Despite children's presence in all areas of society, she states that there are no special considerations for children, even today. Toddlers are expected to wait in supermarket or bank queues with their parents while there are hardly any child-sized toilets or washbasins for them in public places (Leach, 1990). For most children the world remains inaccessible and just out of reach (physically, politically, socially and cognitively). This is because 'in this society children and the people caring for them come last, not first' (p.184).

The structural vulnerability of children is further entrenched by society's tolerance of victimization, such as corporal punishment. Physical punishment is an unpleasant experience for children yet it is still considered by many to be an acceptable and necessary means of discipline (Saunders and Goddard, 1998).

The following quotation from a young person sums up his view of the system's inadequate response to the needs and rights of children who are abused:

> As far as I am concerned, and sorry for saying this, but if you ask me…you know the system is well and truly stuffed… Well, I reckon what should happen, is that the, um, people in the courts should have their bloody consideration right. I reckon us kids should have the right

to be listened to, when or whenever we need to be helped and when we are in danger. (13-year-old male)

Conclusion

The view that children are developmentally 'immature' appears to contribute to their structural vulnerability, and creates confusion and tensions in recognizing children in their own right. Franklin, for example, states that children may be denied participation because of concern for their ability to make informed decisions, and that 'society is attempting nothing more heinous than to protect children from their own incompetence' (1995, p.10). Yet, children demonstrate remarkable ability at decision-making. In sexual abuse, many children 'have to make a complex assessment of the consequences for their family of disclosing that abuse' (Franklin, 1995). This is borne out by what many children in our research said about making disclosures (see Chapter 7). Marshall (1997) strongly asserts that children should not be seen as deviations from adult norms who have to be accommodated into adult-orientated systems. Rather, their rights and needs must be integrated into the system as a whole in order to avoid the sizeable costs associated with child abuse (Daro, 1988; Parton, 1990). Children's civil rights must form the framework against which decisions are made: 'A presumption of competence should prevail and where it is overridden all action should be tested against the promotion and respect for those rights' (Lansdown, 1994, p.44).

CHAPTER 11

The Complexity of Listening Professionally to Children

I mean, people like that are supposed to listen, they're not supposed to sit there and tell you what you're thinking or what you're feeling, because that's what she was doing, just sitting there and telling me what's right.

12-year-old female

Introduction: are we listening to children?

Children's invisibility in child abuse interventions and how their voices were silenced even when they spoke up about their abuse was explored in Chapter 2. The need to listen to children and obtain their views on matters that affect them has therefore been a recurring theme throughout this book. It is also part of an emerging trend to promote children's voices (Butler *et al.*, 2003; Mudaly, 2002; Saunders, 2005; Tucci, 2004). Mullender *et al.* (2002), in their work with children and family violence, assert that children have their own perspectives on what happens to them, that each child reacts as an individual, and that there is no one pattern of responses. They therefore conclude that the perspective of the child must be sought.

Many other authors referred to throughout this book echo a similar sentiment. For this reason, we believe it may be pertinent to briefly reflect upon the concept of listening professionally to children. We do not intend to explore this issue in depth but wish to raise the question about what listening to children in professional interventions might mean. We try to do this in the context of current theoretical constructions and understandings of incorporating children's voices into professional interventions.

Several children in our research talked about the diverse responses they received from professionals (see Chapter 9). Some children felt that professionals did not listen to them (as in the quotation that opens this chapter).

Others felt that the system did not make allowance for their views and experiences to be heard, particularly within the legal system. Some children felt that professionals did not consult them about some interventions. An 18-year-old young person said that she had not been adequately advised on the involvement of child protection services. She also felt that although she had made a statement about her father's sexual abuse of her to the police, they asked *her* to decide about prosecution. This was a decision she felt she was unable to make. These different responses by professionals in the child protection field seem to point to the complexity of listening and responding to children. Yet, if we are to give these children a voice within the child welfare and child protection system, and prevent their continued invisibility and inaudibility, we must know how to listen to them.

The important questions that arise are:

- How do we listen to children?

- How do we incorporate their voices into the work that we do with them?

- How do we interpret and respond to what children say?

Lansdown (1994) is critical of professional attitudes to children, stating that professionals do not make sufficient effort to involve children as participants. Yet, understanding and responding to the voices of children who have been abused is no simple matter. It can be a challenge even for the astute worker who is committed to empowering children and promoting their rights to be heard.

What does listening mean?

The term listen means to 'make an effort to hear something, hear with attention [a] person speaking' (Sykes, 1983, p.588). Translating this into professional practice with children who have been abused challenges this definition in several ways. For example, if a child says he or she wishes to return to an abusive home, does this require the worker to advocate for the child's return home despite concerns for the child's safety?

Littlechild (2000, p.405) reflects upon the complexity of balancing how to effectively give the child the opportunity to have his or her wishes and views directly or indirectly represented in judicial and administrative proceedings. Sometimes professionals who are involved with children from abusive and neglectful families have difficulty working out the most appropriate way to consult these children. There seems to be the desire to promote children's rights to be consulted. Yet many lack the skill to do so sensitively and appropriately. Directly asking children from extremely abusive families 'Where do you wish to live?' can place intense pressure on a child to make a choice about their families. Often this occurs at a time when the child is also experiencing the impact of protective interventions such as being removed from their home and family, in addition to the effects of the abuse.

Children who have been abused may not find it easy to express the conflicting feelings and ideas that they may be experiencing. They may struggle to find the words to fully describe the events that have hurt them and that may be confusing to them (James, 1989). They may have a range of negative feelings that they are unable to name. These may include guilt, or their 'coexistent feelings of love and hate' for a parent who has abused them (James, 1989, p.50).

Such complex emotions may be difficult even for adults to name. McGee (2000, p.220), with reference to children and domestic violence, states that these topics are still 'taboo', and adults, too, do not openly talk about them. The silence around such topics frequently results in children not being taught the relevant language to describe experiences that may be stigmatizing. Therefore listening professionally to children who have been abused and understanding what they say is much more than just hearing their words.

A case study: Amanda's story

Some years ago, the primary author worked with a teenage girl (see Mudaly and Goddard, 2001a). Amanda, a pseudonym chosen by this 13-year-old young person, disclosed sexual abuse by her stepfather. After her disclosure, and subsequent child protection intervention, the stepfather agreed to move out of the home. In the initial months of counselling Amanda repeatedly expressed her wish for her stepfather to return home. But she also did not retract her disclosure and admitted she felt unsafe in his presence during the supervised contact. Understanding what she meant and how best to represent her needs required much professional reflection. It required having to find the balance between giving her an opportunity to be heard and the worker's duty to protect her against further harm (Littlechild, 2000).

The impact of abuse does not only begin after disclosure. The process of victimization (Berliner and Conte, 1990) and the process of offending (see Finkelhor, 1984; Ryan and Lane, 1991; Salter, 1988) begins long before the abuse occurs. Desensitization and 'progressive approximation' to cognitive, emotional and physical acceptance of sexual abuse is a 'gradual sexualisation process' which may take many years of specific grooming of a victim by an offender (Berliner and Conte, 1990, p.18). The victim may develop defences to accommodate and survive this process, and these may be incorporated into the child's personality (MacFarlane *et al.*, 1990; Summit, 1983). This may be a reason why children like Amanda may make contradictory statements: 'Unravelling the web of intra-familial abuse…and understanding the aspects of sexual victimisation which keep children locked in that silent world' requires careful listening and knowledge (MacFarlane *et al.*, 1990 p.155).

In therapy with Amanda, the primary author conveyed to her that what she was hearing her say was that she had been sexually abused by her stepfather; she did not feel safe with him; she felt guilty about the family break-up; and she appeared to want her family to become 'normal' again. Amanda was informed that, based on this assessment, the primary author's recommendation to child protection authorities was that her stepfather not return to the family home. It is not possible to enter into a detailed discussion here about the interventions with Amanda's mother, and the stepfather's counsellor, or the involvement of other professionals here (see Mudaly and Goddard, 2001a). Ultimately, however, Amanda's mother supported her daughter taking the primary author's assessment into consideration, and decided against her husband's returning home. This provided Amanda with the emotional and physical space necessary to work on the impact of the abuse in therapy.

After many months of counselling, Amanda, in a family session with her mother and siblings, confidently verbalized the confusion she had experienced at the beginning of counselling. She admitted to the guilt she had experienced about the impact that her disclosure of abuse had had on her family. She cried as she told them, 'I was so worried about what you all felt about me, blaming me for telling on Dad and for him not being home, so I kept saying I wanted him to come home' (Mudaly and Goddard, 2001a, p.21). She said she had not really wanted him at home and had felt unsafe in his presence for a long time.

This example illustrates that listening to anyone who has been abused is a more complex matter than listening only to what they say. We are certain that there are many professionals who are faced with similar challenges in their work with children who have been abused. Littlechild points to the fact that some children and young people may 'not want the burden of deciding matters but do want their views to be taken into account' (2000, p.408).

Listening to Amanda required 'a broad awareness of sexual abuse issues, research trends, community resources, risk factors for offending, social effects of abuse and disclosure, and offender susceptibilities' (Ryan and Lane, 1991, p.335). This must be the foundation of effective child protection if it is to ensure that children's voices are heard (Bannister, Barrett and Shearer, 1990).

Children's participation: the foundation of listening to them

The concept of children's participation in matters that affect them is deeply embedded in notions of promoting children's rights and, in particular, their right to be heard. There is now much current literature and research on children's participation and the importance of consulting them on matters of practice and policy-making (see, for example, Cairns, 2001; Littlechild, 2000; Reimer, 2003; Sinclair, 2004; Tisdall and Davis, 2004). Many researchers and professionals demonstrate a sincere commitment to promoting children's participation and voices through their research, documenting the hurdles in the process. These include 'addressing attitudinal barriers, creating more participatory structures and processes, achieving inclusive participation, [and] motivating young people to be involved' (Sinclair, 2004, p.114). This was recommended by Lansdown (1994), who stated that to promote real participation by children, one must provide real opportunities for them to express their views by addressing their doubts, confusions and fears, which may impede their participation. It requires listening to their views with respect and seriousness, letting children know how their views will be considered, and keeping them informed of outcomes of decisions and citing full reasons if decisions are negative. It also requires providing them with effective and accessible avenues for their complaints (pp.38–9).

The benefits of listening to children should be apparent. Adults have much to learn from children 'but our assumptions of expertise on the basis of adult status and professional training may prevent us from acknowledging the contribution that children can make' (Atwool, 2000, p.26). The advantages of involving children as partners in matters that affect them are identified by several authors (Healey, 2004; Sinclair, 2004; Weithorn and Scherer, 1994). These include:

- upholding children's rights and recognizing that they are citizens and service users, and therefore share the same fundamental rights to participate

- fulfilling legal responsibilities required by the United Nations Conventions on the Rights of the Child

- allowing children the opportunity to practise making important life decisions; this promotes their growth and development, and they can move into adolescence with confidence, assertiveness and capacities to contribute to democratic dialogue within home, school, community and country

- contributing to children's perception that they have some control over what happens to them

- enabling services to be improved, adapted and made accessible; it also increases children's commitment to and performance in programmes designed for them

- improving decision-making, as children's participation results in more accurate and informed decisions

- increasing children's self-esteem and generating a more positive sense of themselves. Children have shown that, when involved, they can make a difference to the world around them. They have ideas, experience and insights that enrich adult understandings and enhance adult actions.

- involving children is a statement of respect for their individuality and autonomy, and recognizes them as unique persons; it is evident that 'when space is made for them, children's voices express themselves clearly' (Mauthner, 1997, p.21) and the implications for professional interventions are immense.

The views of the children who participated in our research, which are clearly expressed throughout this book, have demonstrated their ability to provide constructive feedback on child protection interventions. It is testimony to the benefits and importance of listening to them. The commitment to promote children's voices through participation is a major step in this direction, an issue we discuss further in the next chapter.

CHAPTER 12

The Way Forward

I am a legend, I will get my life back.

13-year-old male

Introduction

This book has attempted to give a voice to children who have been abused and who have been silenced in various ways. Chapter 2 provided a detailed historical analysis of how children who have been abused have been rendered invisible and inaudible. It explored how early medical research of children, often with very severe injuries, was instrumental in the 'discovery' of child abuse. Yet these children, though central to the research, were 'invisible and inaudible'. They were, in fact, objects for the medical diagnosis of a condition, 'the battered child syndrome' (Kempe *et al.*, 1962). Despite horrific injuries, many children were returned to their abusive homes. Their experiences of abuse, and their needs for protection and care, remained inaudible.

Freeman (2001) reflects on the plight of children in the last millennium. Children were not educated. They were abused, regarded as property and, later, as objects of concern. There appears to be a range of issues that have prompted such responses to children who have been abused. Some of these include controversies about:

- childhood versus adulthood
- children's rights versus adults' rights
- child protection versus family preservation
- children as inherently good and innocent versus evil and bad
- children's needs versus family problems.

These ambivalences and contradictions have guided professional interventions with children who are abused, and continue to be a feature in legislation and policies that affect children.

This book has attempted to demonstrate that children who have been abused are not only visible but, if given the opportunity, can be clearly audible. They do indeed have the ability to eloquently describe their experiences of abuse and their views of professional interventions. Despite perceptions about limitations of their cognitive and emotional ability, the voices of children provide compelling insights and understandings about the dynamics of abuse.

Listening to and taking children seriously is an issue that is beginning to gain widespread attention across different disciplines, especially in regard to the interpretation of childhood (Sidoti, 1999).

The changing concept of childhood

The concept of childhood as an important part of human development, the full extent of child abuse, and the development of children's rights are some of the issues that are currently gaining attention. They are also promoting changes in our relationships with, and views of, children and childhood (Goddard, 1996; Mayall, 1994; Milner and Carolin, 1999; Mullender et. al., 2002). The United Nations Convention on the Rights of the Child (1989) acknowledges children's rights not only to care and protection, but also to be consulted, informed, to participate and be heard in decisions that affect them (Bannister et al., 1990; Goddard, 1996; Milner and Carolin, 1999). Applying these articles in practical terms is, however, a complicated matter, especially in regard to children living with abuse. If we are to respect the principles espoused in the Convention, and give recognition to children's views, we must find a way to listen to and hear what children think, feel and need (Milner and Carolin, 1999). 'Society has to recognise them as real, individual human beings with rights of their own, rather than as appendages of parents who have a right to own them' (Leach, 1990, p.179).

To promote changes to existing structures, attitudes need to change. Bannister et al. (1990, p.xv) state that 'If children are to enjoy the rights accorded to them changes are needed in the way society treats children and the attitudes many adults hold towards children.' Childhood may have been discovered but little has changed for children.

Taking the myth out of adulthood

The adult world is 'not only assumed to be complete, recognizable and in stasis, but also, and perhaps most significantly, desirable' (Jenks, 1996, p.9). It has been regarded not as a stage of human development but the culmination and goal of development (Archard, 1993, p.36). The world of the adult is seen as attractive, the ultimate place to be. The pressure to achieve adulthood comes from all spheres of society. Adulthood attempts to welcome children, by encouraging them to discard the qualities that make them different from adults. It persuades them to assimilate adult processes that would guarantee them adult identities (Jenks, 1996). Adulthood enshrines notions of independence and freedom. Adults have financial freedom and freedom to do as they please. They own cars and houses. Jenks goes on to say that the separation of childhood from adulthood, freeing the child from the adult identity 'has not freed the child from adult society' but 'has made the child subject to new forms of control' by the adult world (p.97). The adult world judges children by adult standards and results in 'miscommunication (with children), inaccurate judgements (about children's intents and motivations), misuse of power (to limit children's self-determination), and undermining strengths and competencies (setting expectations too high or too low)' (Petr, 1998, p.16). While some parents do attempt to listen to their children, Mayall (1999, pp.20–1) states that 'parental agendas, business and authority diminish children's ability to make themselves heard and responded to' within families. Adults also tend to assume that their agendas are more important than children's, and their conceptualization of children as incomplete people 'leads them to downgrade children as moral agents' (Mayall, 1999, p.22). Children's contributions are therefore omitted in the broad spectrum of parents' responsibilities, conceptualizations of adulthood, children and their work.

Legitimizing childhood

Childhood has to be viewed as equal to adulthood if its status is to change. Its specific appeal and place in human development must be legitimized. 'Nature wants children to be children before they are men... Childhood has ways of seeing, thinking, and feeling peculiar to itself: nothing can be more foolish than to substitute our ways for them' (Rousseau, cited in Jenks, 1996, p.3).

Interestingly, children are regarded as our future (Jenks, 1996). 'To abuse a child today is to strike at the remaining embodied vestige of the social bond... The shrill cry of "abuse" is a cry of our own collective pain at the loss of our social identity' (p.109). Yet current statistics on child abuse tell a different story. Children's vulnerabilities need to be seen and accepted as an important and essential feature of childhood if we are to be effective in preventing the abuse of children. According to Summit we need to protect children's vulnerability by understanding 'how exquisitely vulnerable they are' (1990, p.73). The prevention of child abuse therefore should be a major priority, and children's voices are central to this process. Despite abusive and other traumatic experiences, children want to heal and lead healthy lives.

Finding ways to give children a voice is now the subject of much discussion. Children's participation in forums and research are the methods being explored. Encouraging this requires us to address the difficulties associated with children's active participation, and to remove the barriers that prevent children's voices being heard. These include the power relationships (including children's powerless status in society), organizational structures and social inequalities that are a part of our daily lives (James, 2000; Ludbrook, 2001). Grover warns that unless children are allowed to become active participants in the research process, they remain vulnerable to being represented by others, 'just as they are in all other domains of life' (2004, p.92). She states that 'to be in such a position is to have one's own voice silenced and one's fundamental right to be heard effectively quashed' (p.92).

Children who have been abused have to be 'seen' and 'heard'. They must be involved in decision-making. For this to happen, adults have to develop systems that facilitate children's appropriate participation (Marshall, 1997, p.103). This means using children's competencies to promote their engagement in the process. It also requires acknowledgement of their limitations. Such approaches would prevent children being 'accommodated into adult-oriented systems' (p.110) and would ensure that their rights and needs are integrated into the whole system.

In an interesting study by Mayall (1999) involving 57 nine- and twelve-year-old children, she reports on their understandings and experiences of childhood. She states that they 'see themselves as participators in the structuring of their own lives and the lives of their family and friends' (p.19). They see childhood as relational – that is, 'what they are, comes out of relationships' (p.21); in particular, relationships with adults, especially parents and teachers. Contrary to adult perceptions (see Chapter 10), children see themselves as contributing to and participating in family and other relationships that are the cornerstone of their lives. They do so by 'sympathising, caring, worrying, keeping in touch with relatives who live elsewhere and, in particular, of course, fathers' (p.18). They also maintain friendships with peers and act as supports to friends and peers. They describe responsibilities that they hold 'in maintaining the social order of the household' (p.18) by helping with housework and childcare. They also take responsibility for activities related to school and getting work done. These responsibilities are important contributions by children. They need to be acknowledged and accorded serious, if not equal, status to that of the work of adults if we are to change the status of childhood.

Making children visible and audible

To make children visible and audible requires that we address the issues that make them vulnerable to abuse. These were explored in detail in the preceding chapters. The Save the Children organization in the UK (1995, cited in Mayall, 1999, p.26) outlines a number of practical and worthwhile ways to do so. These include the following suggestions.

- The need for child-specific data: this calls for information, facts, and data from children about all aspects of their experiences of life, their social, economic and political conditions, and their understanding and appraisal of childhood.

- The need for recognition of children's productive contribution: children are seen as economic liabilities and a burden to society. Children's productive contributions such as relationship building, as well as paid and unpaid work at home and school, need to be acknowledged to reorientate our thinking about children's place in society.

- The inclusion of children in policy-making: there is need to value and encourage children's participation and decision-making in schools, health centres and support agencies.

- The developing of a more appropriate conceptualization of children and childhood: it is important to be clear about our ideology of childhood and to see children as a social group.

- Gender and generation: children's welfare is generally linked to women's welfare, and women's poverty (a major issue in many countries) has a direct effect on children's welfare. Mothers continue to be the main carers and are also increasingly involved in paid work. Social policies must therefore include resources for children as well as support for mothers to combine paid work with childcare.

Creating a child-centred world

Throughout this book, we have attempted to emphasize the importance of a child-centred approach. A child-centred society that cares for its children and makes children's interests a priority requires an investment in their nurturing, education, health and leisure, irrespective of the capabilities of their parents (Petrie and James, 1995). Such a society is ultimately in everyone's interests. 'Our grandchildren will live together in a society with the offspring of neglected families. So will yours' (Brazelton and Greenspan, 2000, p.ix).

Despite concerted efforts to promote children's rights, to give them a voice and ensure their protection and welfare, 'the plight of children worldwide does not seem to have got any better' (Freeman, 2001, p.i). Freeman lists the millions of children uprooted from their homes and countries, killed, tortured and maimed through wars and political upheavals. Australia, like many other developed countries, prides itself on being a democratic and civilized country. Yet it could do more for children. Protecting children is in some circumstances a specialist activity, but it is also the duty of every citizen (Petrie and James, 1995). Child protection demands the response of national and state governments, communities, business and individuals (Brazelton and Greenspan, 2000).

Australia, where our research was undertaken, has a haphazard history of promoting children's rights and needs. For example, while it ratified the United Nations Convention on the Rights of the Child, it was extremely late in submitting its periodic report. In particular, 'it failed to conduct a proper process of community consultation', necessitating an alternative report after consultations with over 100 non-government agencies (Freeman, 2001, p.iii). This may be an example of Australia paying only lip-service to its commitment to children. It could and should do much more, including appointing a Federal Commissioner for Children. In addition, 'It needs to develop and adopt a National Agenda for Children. It needs to incorporate the United Nations Convention on the Rights of the Child into Australian law or, better still, improve upon this with its own Children's Act' (Freeman, 2001, p.v).

Developing a way of thinking about children, an attitude and a belief system that inherently values children, is a principle that must be shared by all adults the world over. It should be an issue that unites rather than divides societies, countries and individuals. The long-term value of such an approach cannot be underestimated. The current suffering of children from poverty and starvation, from wars and political turmoil, from exploitation for labour, sex and slavery, from domestic violence and abuse, and from being held under inhumane conditions in detention centres (see, for example, Goddard and Briskman, 2004), should not be tolerated by a civilized and caring society.

These are the children who will be the citizens of tomorrow, caring for future generations of children. Nurturing children and accepting them as legitimate members of this world, and the most valuable citizens of society, may lead to a world that is founded on respect, gentleness and empathy. To be truly child centred would ultimately change our attitudes and relationships with each other and with our children. This should surely be an international priority. The truth about child abuse, and childhood itself, is indeed longer than a lie.

References

Alderson, P. (1995) *Listening to Children. Children, Ethics and Social Research.* Barkingside: Barnardo's.

Amaya-Jackson, L., Socolar, R.R.S., Hunter, W., Runyan, D.K. and Colindres, R. (2000) 'Directly questioning children and adolescents about maltreatment. A review of survey measures used.' *Journal of Interpersonal Violence 15,* 7, 725–59.

Ammerman, R. T. and Hersen, M. (eds) (1990) *Children at Risk. An Evaluation of Factors Contributing to Child Abuse and Neglect.* New York: Plenum Press.

Angus, G. and Wilkinson, K. (1993) *Child Abuse and Neglect in Australia 1990–91.* Australian Institute of Health and Welfare: Child Welfare Series No. 2. AGPS: Canberra.

Archard, D. (1993) *Children: Rights and Childhood.* London: Routledge.

Ariès, P. (1962) *Centuries of Childhood.* London: Cape.

Atwool, N. (2000) 'Trauma and children's rights.' In A.B. Smith, M. Gollop, K. Marshall and K. Nairn (eds) *Advocating for Children. International Perspectives on Children's Rights.* Dunedin, New Zealand: University of Otago Press, 19–31.

Australian Childhood Foundation. (2003) Practice Framework. Melbourne, Australia: Australian Childhood Foundation.

Australians Against Child Abuse (2001) Practice Framework. Melbourne, Australia: Australian Childhood Foundation.

Bandura, A. (1990) 'Mechanisms of moral disengagement. Psychologies, ideologies, theologies, states of mind.' In W. Reich (ed.) *Origins of Terrorism.* Cambridge. Woodrow Wilson International Centre for Scholars and Cambridge University Press, 161–91.

Bannister, A. (1990) 'Listening and learning: psychodramatic techniques with children.' In A. Bannister, K. Barrett and E. Shearer (eds) *Listening to Children: The Professional Response to Hearing the Abused Child.* Essex: Longman, 155–70.

Bannister, A., Barrett, K. and Shearer, E. (eds) (1990) *Listening to Children: The Professional Response to Hearing the Abused Child.* Essex: Longman.

Belsky, J. (1978) 'Three theoretical models of child abuse: a critical review.' *Child Abuse and Neglect 2,* 1, 37–49.

Benedict, H. (1992) *Virgin or Vamp. How the Press Covers Sex Crimes.* New York: Oxford University Press.

Bentovim, A. (2002) 'Preventing sexually abused young people from becoming abusers, and treating the victimization experiences of young people who offend sexually.' *Child Abuse and Neglect 26,* 661–78.

Berg, B.L. (1998) *Qualitative Research Methods for the Social Sciences* (3rd edn). Boston: Allyn & Bacon.

Berglund, C. A. (1995) 'Children in medical research: Australian ethical standards.' *Child Care, Health and Development 21*, 2, 149–59.

Berliner, L. and Conte, J.R. (1990) 'The process of victimisation: The Victim's Perspective.' *Child Abuse & Neglect 14*, 29–40.

Berry, J. (1972) *Social Work with Children.* London: Routledge.

Bialestock, D. (1966) 'Neglected babies: A study of 289 babies admitted consecutively to a reception centre.' *Medical Journal of Australia 2*, 1129–33.

Birrell, R.G. and Birrell, J.H.W. (1966) 'The "Maltreatment Syndrome" in Children.' *Medical Journal of Australia 2*, 1134–38.

Black, M.M and Ponirakis, A. (2000) 'Computer-administered interviews with children about maltreatment: Methodological, developmental, and ethical issues.' *Journal of Interpersonal Violence 15*, 7, 682–95.

Bowes, J. and Watson, J. (1999) 'Families as a context for children.' In J.M. Bowes and A. Hayes (eds) *Children, Families, and Communities. Contexts and Consequences.* Melbourne, Australia: Oxford University Press, 76–93.

Bowlby, J. (1967) *Child Care and the Growth of Love.* London: Penguin Books.

Bray, M. and Pugh, R. (1997) 'Listening to children: Appreciating the abused child's reality.' In J. Bates, R. Pugh and N. Thompson (eds) *Protecting Children: Challenges and Change.* London: Arena, 143–56.

Brazelton, T.B. (MD) and Greenspan S.I. (MD) (2000) *The Irreducible Needs of Children. What Every Child Must Have to Grow, Learn, and Flourish.* Cambridge: Perseus Publishing.

Briere, J. (1992) *Child Abuse Trauma. Theory and Treatment of the Lasting Effects.* Newbury Park: Sage Publications.

Briere, J. (2004) 'Treating long-term effects of childhood maltreatment: a brief overview.' *Psychotherapy in Australia 10*, 3, 12–19.

Brock, E. (1993) 'On becoming a tightrope walker. Communicating effectively with children about abuse.' In H. Owen and J. Pritchard (eds) *Good Practice in Child Protection. A Manual for Professionals.* London: Jessica Kingsley Publishers, 113–24.

Browne, K. (1995) 'Child Abuse: Defining, understanding and intervening.' In K. Wilson and A. James (eds) *The Child Protection Handbook.* London: Balliere Tindall, 43–65.

Browne, K., Davies, C. and Stratton, P. (1988) *Early Prediction and Prevention of Child Abuse.* Chichester: John Wiley and Sons.

Butcher, S. (2005) 'Girl tried suicide after judge's grilling.' *The Age.* Melbourne, Australia, 23 May, pp.1–2.

Butler, I., Scanlan, L., Robinson, G.D. and Murch, M. (2003) *Divorcing Children. Children's Experiences of Their Parents' Divorce.* London: Jessica Kingsley Publishers.

Cairns, L. (2001) 'Investing in children: Learning how to promote the rights of all children.' *Children & Society 15*, 347–60.

Calam, R. and Franchi, C. (1987) *Child Abuse and its Consequences: Observational Approaches.* Cambridge: Cambridge University Press.

Cameron, D (ed.) (1990) *The Feminist Critique of Language: A Reader.* London: Routledge.

Cashmore, J. and Bussey, K. (1988) 'Disclosure of child sexual abuse: Issues for a child-oriented perspective.' *Australian Journal of Social Issues 23*, 1, 13–26.

Centre for Children (1999) *Information for Referral Agencies.* Melbourne: Australians Against Child Abuse.

Christensen, P.H. (2004) 'Children's participation in ethnographic research: Issues of power and representation.' *Children and Society 18*, 165–76.

Clark, M. (1986) *A Short History of Australia.* Ringwood: Penguin.

Cloke, C. and Davies, M. (eds) (1995) *Participation and Empowerment in Child Protection.* London: Pitman.

Cooke, R.E. (1994) 'Vulnerable children.' In M.A. Grodin and L.H. Glantz (eds) *Children as Research Subjects.* New York: Oxford University Press, 193–214.

Corby, B. (1993) *Child Abuse: Towards a Knowledge Base.* Buckingham: Open University Press.

Cordes, B. (1987) 'Euroterrorists talk about themselves: a look at the literature.' In P. Wilkinson and A.M. Stewart, *Contemporary Research on Terrorism.* Aberdeen: University Press, 318–36.

Crayton, J.W. (1983) 'Terrorism and the psychology of the self.' In L.Z. Freedman and Y. Alexander (eds) *Perspectives on Terrorism.* Wilmington, Delaware: Scholarly Resources Inc., 33–41.

Crelinsten, R.D. (1987) 'Terrorism as political communication: The relationship between the controller and the controlled.' In P. Wilkinson and A.M. Stewart (eds) *Contemporary Research on Terrorism.* Aberdeen: University Press, 3–23.

Dale, P., Davies, M., Morrison, T. and Waters, J. (1986) *Dangerous Families. Assessment and Treatment of Child Abuse.* London: Tavistock.

Daro, D. (1988) *Confronting Child Abuse: Research for Effective Program Design.* New York: The Free Press.

De Mause, L. (1974) *The History of Childhood.* New York: Psychohistory Press.

Denzin, N.K. and Lincoln, Y.S. (eds) (2000) *Handbook of Qualitative Research* (2nd edn) London: Sage Publications Inc.

Desivilya, H.S., Gal, R. and Ayalon, O. (1996) 'Long-term effects of trauma in adolescence. Comparison between survivors of a terrorist attack and control counterparts.' *Anxiety, Stress & Coping: An Interpersonal Journal 9*, 2, 135–50.

Doyle, C. (1990) *Working with Abused Children.* Basingstoke: Macmillan.

Doyle, C. (1997a) *Working with Abused Children* (2nd edn) Basingstoke: Macmillan.

Doyle, C. (1997b) 'Terror and the Stockholm Syndrome: The relevance for abused children.' In J. Bates, R. Pugh and N. Thompson (eds) *Protecting Children: Challenges and Change.* Aldershot: Arena, 103–14.

Doyle, R. (1993) *Paddy Clarke Ha Ha Ha.* London: Secker and Warburg.

Edwards, R. and Alldred, P. (1999) 'Children and young people's views of social research. The case of research on home–school relations.' *Childhood 6*, 2, 261–81.

Ellingsen, P. (2005) 'New law to ease court ordeal for sex victims.' *The Sunday Age.* Melbourne, Australia, 22 May, pp.1–20.

Emmison, M. and Smith, P. (2000) *Researching the Visual. Images, Objects, Contexts and Interaction in Social and Cultural Inquiry.* London: Sage Publications.

Factor, D.C. and Wolfe, D.A. (1990) 'Parental psychopathology and high-risk children.' In R.T. Ammerman and M. Hersen (eds) *Children at Risk. An Evaluation of Factors Contributing to Child Abuse and Neglect.* New York: Plenum Press, 171–98.

Fairclough, N. (1992) *Discourse and Social Change.* Cambridge: Polity Press.

Fairclough, N. (1995) *Critical Discourse Analysis: The Critical Study of Language.* London: Longman.

Fields, R.M. (1982) 'Research on victims of terrorism.' In F.M. Ochberg and D.A. Soskis (eds) *Victims of Terrorism.* Boulder, Colorado: Westview Press, 137–48.

Fine, G.A. and Sandstrom, K.L. (1988) *Knowing Children: Participant Observation with Minors.* Newbury Park, California: Sage Publications.

Finkelhor, D. (1984) *Child Sexual Abuse: New Theory and Research.* New York: The Free Press.

Finkelhor, D. (1994) 'The victimisation of children in a developmental perspective.' Paper presented at ISPCAN Conference, August, Malaysia.

Finkelhor, D. (1997) 'The victimisation of children and youth. Developmental victimology.' In R.C. Davis, A.J. Lurigio and W.G. Skogan (eds) *Victims of Crime* (2nd edn). Thousand Oaks, CA: Sage Publications, Inc., 86–107.

Flick, U. (1998) An Introduction to Qualitative Research. London: Sage Publications.

Flynn, E.E. (1987) 'Victims of Terrorism: Dimensions of the Victim Experience.' In P. Wilkinson and A.M. Stewart (eds) *Contemporary Research on Terrorism.* Aberdeen: University Press, 337–55.

Forward, S. (1989) *Toxic Parents: Overcoming their Hurtful Legacy and Reclaiming your Life.* New York: Bantam.

France, A., Bendelow, G. and Williams, S. (2000) 'A 'risky' business: researching the health beliefs of children and young people.' In A. Lewis and G. Lindsay (eds) *Researching Children's Perspectives.* Buckingham: Open University Press.

Franklin, B. (1986) *The Rights of Children.* Oxford: Basil Blackwell.

Franklin, B. (1995) 'The case for children's rights: a progress report.' In B. Franklin (ed.) *The Handbook of Children's Rights. Comparative Policy and Practice.* London: Routledge, 3–21.

Franklin, B. (2001) 'Children's rights and medial wrongs: changing representations of children and the developing rights agenda.' In B. Franklin (ed.) *The New Handbook of Children's Rights. Comparative Policy and Practice.* London: Routledge, 15–42.

Franklin, B. and Parton, N. (eds) (1991) *Social Work, the Media, and Public Relations.* London and New York: Routledge.

Freeman, M. (2001) 'Foreword: Recognising a child's humanity.' In M. Jones and L.A. Basser Marks *Children on the Agenda: The Rights of Australia's Children.* St Leonards, NSW: Prospect Media Pty, Ltd, i–v.

Gandevia, B. (1978) *Tears Often Shed: Child Health and Welfare in Australia from 1788.* Gordon, NSW: Charter Books.

Garbarino, J., Guttman, E. and Seeley, J.M. (1986) *The Psychologically Battered Child.* California: Jossey-Bass Publishers.

Geldard, K. and Geldard, D. (1997) *Counselling Children: A Practical Introduction.* London: Sage Publications.

Gelles, R.J. (1993) 'Family Violence.' In R.L. Hampton, T.P. Gullotta, G.R. Adams, E.H. Potter III and R.P. Weissberg (eds) *Family Violence: Prevention and Treatment.* Newbury Park, CA: Sage Publications, 1–24.

Gil, D.G. (1975) 'Unravelling child abuse.' *American Journal of Orthopsychiatry 45*, 3, 346–56.

Gilligan, P. (1994) 'Child centred practice: The core components.' *Journal of Child Centred Practice 1*, 2, 119–24.

Glantz, L.H. (1996) 'Conducting research with children: Legal and ethical issues.' *Journal of the American Academy of Child and Adolescent Psychiatry 35*, 10, 1283–91.

Goddard, C. (1981) *Child Abuse: A Hospital Study.* Master of Social Work by Research Thesis. Monash University.

Goddard, C. (1988) 'Social workers' responses to repeated hostility in child abuse cases. The traditional social worker-client relationship or a new approach to hostage theory?' *Proceedings of the First Victorian Conference on Child Abuse. Facing the Future.* Melbourne, Australia: VicSPCAN, 146–63.

Goddard, C. (1993) 'Daniel's day in court.' *The Age.* Melbourne, Australia, 22 November, p.11.

Goddard, C. (1996) *Child Abuse and Child Protection: A Guide for Health, Education and Welfare Workers.* Melbourne, Australia: Churchill Livingstone.

Goddard, C. (2000) 'A case of repeated abuse.' *The Age,* Melbourne, Australia, 23 June, p.15.

Goddard, C. (2003) 'A role fit for Hollingworth.' *The Age.* Melbourne, Australia, 6 May, p.17.

Goddard, C. (2004) 'We must rise up against the globalisation of child pornography.' *The Age.* Melbourne, Australia, 15 October, p.15.

Goddard, C. and Briskman, L. (2004) 'By any Measure, it's Official Child Abuse.' *Herald Sun.* Melbourne, Australia, 19 February, p.17.

Goddard, C. and Carew, R. (1993) *Responding to Children: Child Welfare Practice.* Melbourne, Australia: Longman Cheshire.

Goddard, C. and Hiller, P. (1993a) 'Child sexual abuse: assault in a violent context.' *Australian Journal of Social Issues 28*, 1, 20–33.

Goddard, C. and Hiller, P. (1993b) 'The minimisation of child abuse and neglect: The role of the police, the courts, and protective services.' Paper presented at the 3rd Asian Conference on Child Abuse and Neglect: 'Child Abuse and Neglect: Asian Perspectives', 5–12 January.

Goddard, C. and Liddell, M. (1995) 'Child abuse fatalities and the media: Lessons from a case study.' *Child Abuse Review 4,* 356–64.

Goddard, C. and Mudaly, N. (2003) 'Listen to the children.' *The Age.* Melbourne, Australia, 28 October, p.13.

Goddard, C. and Saunders, B.J. (2000) 'The gender neglect and textual abuse of children in the print media.' *Child Abuse Review 9,* 37–48.

Goddard, C. and Stanley, J.R (1994) 'Viewing the abusive parent and the abused child as captor and hostage: The application of the hostage theory to the effects of child abuse.' *Journal of Interpersonal Violence 9*, 2, 258–69.

Goddard, C. and Tucci, J. (2004) 'The short life and death of Jed Britton.' *The Age.* Melbourne, Australia, 11 July, p.13.

Goddard, C., de Bortoli, L., Saunders, B.J. and Tucci, J. (2005) 'The rapist's camouflage: 'Child prostitution'.' *Child Abuse Review 14*, 275–291.

Gordon, L. (1990) *Taking Child Abuse Seriously. Contemporary Issues in Child Protection Theory and Practice.* London: Unwin Hyman.

Greer, G. (1984) *Sex and Destiny. The Politics of Human Fertility.* London: Secker & Warburg.

Grinnell, R.M. Jr (1993) *Social Work Research and Evaluation* (4th edn). Itasca, Illinois: F.E Peacock Publishers.

Grinnell, R.M. Jr (1997) *Social Work Research and Evaluation: Quantitative and Qualitative Approaches* (5th edn). Itasca, Illinois: F.E Peacock Publishers.

Grover, S. (2004) 'Why won't they listen to us? On giving power and voice to children participating in social research.' *Childhood 11*, 1, 81–93.

Hanks, H. and Stratton, P. (1995) 'The effects of child abuse: Signs and symptoms.' In K. Wilson and A. James (eds) *The Child Protection Handbook.* London: Balliere Tindall, 84–107.

Harmon, C.C. (2000) *Terrorism Today.* London: Frank Cass Publishers.

Hatcher, C. (1987) 'A conceptual framework in victimology: The adult and child hostage experience.' In P. Wilkinson and A.M. Stewart (eds) *Contemporary Research on Terrorism.* Aberdeen: University Press, 357–75.

Healey, J. (ed.) (2004) *Children's Rights. Issues in Society.* Vol. 198. Sydney: The Spinney Press.

Heger, A., Ticson, L., Velasquez, O. and Bernier, R. (2002) 'Children referred for possible sexual abuse: medical findings in 2384 children.' *Child Abuse Review 26*, 645–59.

Herman, J.L. (1992) *Trauma and Recovery.* London: Pandora.

Hill, M. (1997) 'Participatory research with children.' *Child and Family Social Work 2*, 171–83.

Howe, D. (1996) 'Attachment theory in child and family social work.' In D. Howe, *Attachment and Loss in Child and Family Social Work.* Aldershot: Avebury, 1–17.

Howitt, D. (1992) *Child abuse errors: When good intentions go wrong.* New York: Harvester Wheatsheaf.

Hoyles, M. and Evans, P. (1989) *The Politics of Childhood.* London: Journeyman Press.

Hudson, W.W. and Nurius, P.S. (eds) (1994) *Controversial Issues in Social Work Research.* Boston. Allyn & Bacon.

Hughes, D.A. (1997) *Facilitating Developmental Attachment. The Road to Emotional Recovery and Behavioural Change in Foster and Adopted Children.* New Jersey: Jason Aronson Inc.

Hughes, D.A. (2005) *Dyadic Developmental Psychotherapy.* Workshop handout. March. Melbourne, Victoria.

Hutchby, I. and Wooffitt, R. (1998) *Conversation Analysis: Principles, Practices and Applications*. Cambridge: Polity Press.

Irwin, H.J. (1998) 'Childhood trauma and the development of a dissociative coping style.' *Journal of Child Centred Practice 5*, 2, 95–104.

James, A. (2000) 'Researching children: the way ahead in theory and in practice.' In J. Mason and M. Wilkinson, *Taking Children Seriously. Proceedings of a National Workshop, 12–13 July 1999*. Western Sydney: Childhood and Youth Policy Research Unit, 171–87.

James, A., Jenks, C. and Prout, A. (1998) *Theorizing Childhood*. Cambridge: Polity Press.

James, B. (1989) *Treating Traumatised Children: New Insights and Creative Interventions*. New York: Lexington Books.

James, M. (1994) 'Domestic violence as a form of child abuse: Identification and prevention.' *Issues in Child Abuse Prevention 2*.

Janesick, V.J. (2000) 'The choreography of qualitative research design: minuets, improvisations, and crystallization.' In N.K. Denzin and Y.S. Lincoln (eds) *Handbook of Qualitative Research* (2nd edn). London: Sage Publications Inc., 379–99.

Jenks, C. (1996) *Childhood*. London: Routledge.

Jones, D.N., Pickett, J., Oates, M.R. and Barbor, P.R.H. (1987) *Understanding Child Abuse*. London: Macmillan Education.

Jones, D.P.H. (1990) 'Talking with children.' In K. R. Oates (ed) *Understanding and Managing Child Sexual Abuse*. London: Balliere Tindall W.B. Saunders, 97–115.

Jones, D.P.H. and Ramchandani, P. (1999) *Child Sexual Abuse. Informing Practice from Research*. Oxon: Radcliffe Medical Press.

Kellehear, A. (1993) *The Unobtrusive Researcher. A Guide to Methods*. New South Wales: Allan & Unwin.

Kempe, C.H., Silverman, F.N., Steele, B.F., Droegemueller, W. and Silver, H.K. (1962) 'The battered-child syndrome.' *Journal of the American Medical Association 181*, 1, 17–24.

Kenward, H. and Hevey, D. (1992) 'The effects of physical abuse and neglect.' In W.S. Rogers, D. Hevey, J. Roche and E. Ash (eds) *Child Abuse and Neglect: Facing the Challenge*. London: B.T. Batsford Ltd, 203–9.

Kinard, E.M. (1985) 'Ethical issues in research with abused children.' *Child Abuse & Neglect 9*, 301–11.

King, M. (1997) *A Better World for Children: Explorations in Morality and Authority*. London: Routledge.

King, N.M.P. and Churchill, L.R. (2000) 'Ethical principles guiding research on child and adolescent subjects.' *Journal of Interpersonal Violence 15*, 7, 710–24.

Kinsey, A.C., Pomeroy, W.B., Martin, C.E., and Gebhard, P.H. (1953) *Sexual Behaviour in the Human Female*. Philadelphia and London: W.B. Saunders.

Kluft, E.S. (1998) 'A literary overview of multiple personality disorder.' In E.S. Kluft (ed.) *Expressive and Functional Therapies in the Treatment of Multiple Personality Disorder*. Springfield: Charles C. Thomas Publisher, 3–22.

Koocher, G.P. and Keith-Spiegel, P. (1994) 'Scientific issues in psychosocial and educational research with children.' In M.A. Grodin and L.H. Glantz (eds) *Children as Research Subjects. Science, Ethics and the Law.* New York: Oxford University Press, 47–80.

Korbin, J.E. (1987) 'Child abuse and neglect: The cultural context.' In R.E. Helfer and R.S. Kempe (eds) *The Battered Child* (4th edn). Chicago: University of Chicago Press, 23–41.

Lansdown, G. (1994) 'Children's rights.' In B. Mayall (ed.) *Children's Childhoods. Observed and Experienced.* London: Falmer Press.

Leach, P. (1990) 'Towards a child-friendly society.' In A. Bannister, K. Barrett and E. Shearer (eds) *Listening to Children. The Professional Response to Hearing the Abused Child.* Essex, UK: Longman, 172–84.

Leonard, M. (2005) *Involving Children in Social Policy: A Case Study from Northern Ireland.* Presentation on 24 February at the Australian Institute of Family Studies, Melbourne.

Liddell, M. and Goddard, C. (2005) 'Australian governments protecting children in detention: A View through the Looking Glass.' *Children Australia 30*, 1, 11–18.

Lincoln, Y.S. and Guba, E.G. (2000) 'Paradigmatic controversies, contradictions, and emerging confluences.' In N.K. Denzin and Y.S. Lincoln (eds) *Handbook of Qualitative Research* (2nd edn). London: Sage Publications Inc., 163–88.

Littlechild, B. (2000) 'Children's rights to be heard in child protection processes – Law, Policy and Practice in England and Wales.' *Child Abuse Review 9*, 403–15.

Lord Laming (2003) *The Victoria Climbié Inquiry: Report of an Inquiry by Lord Laming.* London: The Stationery Office.

Ludbrook, R. (2001) 'Children and the political process.' In M. Jones and L.A. Basser Marks, *Children on the Agenda: The Rights of Australia's Children.* St Leonards, NSW: Prospect Media Pty, Ltd, 65–87.

MacFarlane, K., Cockriel, M. and Dugan, M. (1990) 'Treating young victims of incest.' In K.R. Oates (ed.) *Understanding and Managing Child Sexual Abuse.* Sydney, Australia: Harcourt Brace Jovanovich, 149–77.

Macklin, R. (1992) 'Autonomy, beneficence, and child development: An ethical analysis.' In B. Stanley and J. E. Sieber (eds) *Social Research on Children and Adolescents.* Newbury Park: Sage Publications, 88–108.

Mannarino, A.P. and Cohen, J.A. (1990) 'Treating the abused child.' In R.T. Ammerman and M. Hersen (eds) *Children at Risk: An Evaluation of Factors Contributing to Child Abuse and Neglect.* New York: Plenum Press, 249–68.

Marshall, C. and Rossman, G.B. (1995) *Designing Qualitative Research* (2nd edn). Thousand Oaks: Sage Publications.

Marshall, K. (1997) *Children's Rights in the Balance: The Participation–Protection Debate.* Edinburgh: The Stationery Office Ltd.

Mason, J. (1999) 'Taking children seriously: some policy implications for children protection policy and practice.' Keynote paper. In J. Mason and M. Wilkinson (eds) *Taking Children Seriously. Proceedings of a National Workshop,* 12–13 July. University of Western Sydney Macarthur. Childhood and Youth Policy Research Unit, Australia, 27–41.

Mauthner, M. (1997) 'Methodological aspects of collecting data from children. Lessons from three research projects.' *Children and Society 11,* 1, 16–28.

Mayall, B. (ed.) (1994) *Children's Childhoods: Observed and Experienced.* London: Falmer Press.

Mayall, B. (1999) 'The social condition of UK childhoods: children's understandings and their implications.' Keynote address. In J. Mason and M. Wilkinson (eds) *Taking Children Seriously. Proceedings of a National Workshop,* 12–13 July. University of Western Sydney Macarthur. Childhood and Youth Policy Research Unit, Australia, 9–26.

McGee, C. (2000) *Childhood Experiences of Domestic Violence.* London: Jessica Kingsley Publishers.

Melton, G.B. (1992) 'Respecting boundaries: Minors, privacy, and behavioural research.' In B. Stanley and J.E. Sieber (eds) *Social Research on Children and Adolescents.* Newbury Park: Sage Publications, 65–87.

Miller, A.H. (1980) *Terrorism and Hostage Negotiations.* Boulder, Colorado: Westview Press.

Milner, P. and Carolin, B. (eds) (1999) *Time to Listen to Children.* London: Routledge.

Minichiello, V., Aroni, R., Timewell, E. and Alexander, L. (1995) *In-depth Interviewing. Principles, Techniques, Analysis* (2nd edn). Melbourne: Longman.

Morrow, V. and Richards, M. (1996) 'The ethics of social research with children. An overview.' *Children & Society 10,* 2, 90–105.

Mudaly, N. (1998) *'Getting our Lives Back'. Young People's Experiences of Child Abuse and Their Perception of Their Future.* Paper presented at the Kids First Agenda for Change National Conference. Melbourne, Victoria.

Mudaly, N. (2001) *No Way Out: Exploration of the Hostage Theory in Relation to Children's Abusive Experiences.* Paper presented at the Eight Australasian Conference on Child Abuse and Neglect. Melbourne, Victoria.

Mudaly, N. (2002) *Listening to Children who have been Abused. What They Tell us About Abuse and Professional Interventions.* PhD thesis. Melbourne: Monash University.

Mudaly, N. and Goddard, C. (2001a) 'Listening to the child victim of abuse through the process of therapy. A case study.' *Children Australia 26,* 3, 18–22.

Mudaly, N. and Goddard, C. (2001b) 'The child abuse victim as a hostage: Scorpion's story.' *Child Abuse Review 10,* 428–39.

Mullender, A., Hague, G., Imam, U., Kelly, L., Malos, E. and Regan, l. (2002) *Children's Perspectives on Domestic Violence.* London: Sage Publications.

Mullens, P. and Fleming, J. (1998) *Long Term Effects of Child Sexual Abuse.* Issues Paper No. 9. Melbourne: National Child Protection Clearinghouse.

Murphy, M. (1995) *Working Together in Child Protection. An Exploration of the Multi-disciplinary Task and System.* Aldershot: Arena.

Nelson, B.J. (1984) *Making an Issue of Child Abuse: Political Agenda-setting for Social Problems.* Chicago: University of Chicago Press.

Neuman, L.W. (1997) *Social Research Methods. Qualitative and Quantitative Approaches* (3rd edn). Boston: Allyn & Bacon.

Oaklander, V. (1988) *Windows to our Children. A Gestalt Therapy Approach to Children and Adolescents*. New York: The Gestalt Journal Press.

Oaklander, V. (1997) 'The Therapeutic Process with Children and Adolescents.' *Gestalt Review 1*, 4, 292–317.

Padgett, D.K. (1998) *Qualitative Methods in Social Work Research. Challenges and Rewards*. Thousand Oaks: Sage Publications.

Parton, N. (1990) 'Taking child abuse seriously.' In Violence Against Children Study Group, *Taking Child Abuse Seriously: Contemporary Issues in Child Protection Theory and Practice*. London: Unwin Hyman, 7–24.

Parton, N. (2004) 'From Maria Colwell to Victoria Climbié: Reflections on public inquiries into child abuse a generation apart.' *Child Abuse Review 13*, 30–94.

Pease, L. and Goddard, C. (1996) 'Chapters in a collective biography of child sexual abuse.' *Australian Social Work 49*, 2, 11–17.

Peled, E. and Leichtentritt, R. (2002) 'The Ethics of Social Work Research.' *Qualitative Social Work. Research and Practice 1*, 2, 145–69.

Perry, B.D. (1996) 'Neurodevelopmental adaptations to violence: How children survive the intragenerational vortex of violence.' In Urban Child Research Center, *Violence and Childhood Trauma: Understanding and Responding to the Effects of Violence on Young Children*. Cleveland, Ohio: Gund Foundation.

Perry, B.D. (2000) *Violence and Childhood: How Persisting Fear can Alter the Developing Child's Brain*. Houston, Texas: The Child Trauma Academy.

Peterson, C. (1996) *Looking Forward Through the Lifespan* (3rd edn). Sydney: Prentice Hall.

Petr, C.G. (1998) *Social Work with Children and their Families*. Oxford: Oxford University Press.

Petrie, A. and James, A.L. (1995) 'Partnership with parents.' In K. Wilson and A. James (eds) *The Child Protection Handbook*. London: Balliere Tindall, 313–33.

Post, J.M. (1990) 'Terrorist Psycho-logic: Terrorist behaviour as a product of psychological forces.' In W. Reich (ed.) *Origins of Terrorism*. Cambridge: Woodrow Wilson International Centre for Scholars and Cambridge University Press, 25–40.

Psathas, G. (1990) 'Introduction: Methodological issues in recent developments in the study of naturally occurring interaction.' In G. Psathas (ed.) *Interaction Competence*. Washington DC: University Press of America, 1–29.

Psathas, G. (1995) *Conversation Analysis. The Study of Talk-in-interaction*. Thousand Oaks: Sage Publications.

Radbill, S.X. (1980) 'Children in a World of Violence: A History of Child Abuse.' In C.H. Kempe and R.E. Helfer (eds) *The Battered Child* (3rd edn). Chicago: University of Chicago Press, 3–20.

Reder, P., Duncan, S. and Gray, M. (1993) *Beyond Blame: Child Abuse Tragedies Revisited*. London: Routledge.

Reimer, E.C. (2003) 'A scaffold for participation in agency work.' *Children Australia 28*, 3, 30–37.

Ross, E.M. (1990) 'Learning to listen to children.' In A. Bannister, K. Barrett and E. Shearer (eds) *Listening to Children: The Professional Response to Hearing the Abused Child*. Essex, UK: Longman, 100-109.

Runyan, D.K. (2000) 'Introduction: The ethical, legal, and methodological implications of directly asking children about abuse.' *Journal of Interpersonal Violence 15*, 7, 675–81.

Rush, F. (1980) *The Best Kept Secret: Sexual Abuse of Children.* Englewood Cliffs, New Jersey: Prentice-Hall.

Ryan, G.D. and Lane, S.L. (eds) (1991) *Juvenile Sexual Offending. Causes, Consequences and Corrections.* Lexington: Lexington Books, D.C. Heath and Co.

Salter, A (1988) *Treating Child Sex Offenders and Victims.* London: Sage Publications.

Sanders, R. (1999) *The Management of Child Protection Services. Context and Change.* Aldershot: Ashgate Publishing Co.

Saunders, B. (2005) '*Because There's a Better Way than Hurting Someone'. Children, Parents, Grandparents and Professionals Share Their Experiences of, and Views About, Physical Punishment in Childhood.* Monash University, PhD thesis.

Saunders, B. and Goddard, C. (1998) *Why Do We Condone the Physical Punishment of Children by Parents and Carers?* Melbourne: Child Abuse and Family Violence Research Unit and Australians Against Child Abuse.

Saunders, B. and Goddard, C. (2001) 'The textual abuse of childhood in the English-speaking world: The contribution of language to the denial of children's rights.' *Childhood: A Global Journal Of Child Research 8*, 443–62.

Saunders, B. and Goddard, C. (2005) 'The objectification of the child through "physical discipline" and language. The debate on children's rights continues.' In J. Mason and R. Fattore, *Children Taken Seriously. In Theory, Policy and Practice.* London: Jessica Kingsley Publishers, 113–22.

Schaefer, C.E. and Cangelosi, D.M. (eds) (1993) *Play Therapy Techniques.* New Jersey: Jason Aronson Inc.

Sidoti, C. (1999) 'Taking children seriously.' Opening address. In J. Mason and M. Wilkinson (eds) *Taking Children Seriously. Proceedings of a National Workshop,* 12–13 July. University of Western Sydney Macarthur. Childhood and Youth Policy Research Unit. Australia, 1–8.

Sinclair, R. (2004) 'Participation in Practice: Making it meaningful, effective and sustainable.' *Children & Society 18*, 106–18.

Smedley, B. (1999) 'Child Protection.' In P. Milner and B. Carolin (eds) *Time to Listen to Children.* London: Routledge, 112–25.

Soskis, D.A. and Ochberg, F.M. (1982) 'Concepts of terrorist victimization.' In F.M. Ochberg and D.A. Soskis (eds) *Victims of Terrorism.* Boulder, Colorado: Westview Press, 105–35.

Sroufe, L.A., Cooper R.G. and DeHart G.B. (1992) *Child Development. Its Nature and Course (2nd edn).* New York: McGraw-Hill Inc.

Stanley, B. and Sieber, J.E. (1992) *Social Research on Children and Adolescents: Ethical Issues.* Newbury Park: Sage Publications.

Stanley, J. (2001) 'Child abuse and the internet.' *Child Abuse Prevention Issues,* no. 15. Melbourne: National Child Protection Clearinghouse.

Stanley, J.R. and Goddard, C.R. (1993a) 'The association between child abuse and other family violence.' *Australian Social Work 46*, 2, 3–8.

Stanley, J.R. and Goddard, C.R. (1993b) 'The effect of child abuse and other family violence on the child protection worker and case management.' *Australian Social Work 46*, 3, 1–8.

Stanley, J.R. and Goddard, C.R. (1995) 'The abused child as a hostage. Insights from the hostage theory on pathological attachment and some developmental implications.' *Children Australia 20*, 1, 24–9.

Stanley, J.R. and Goddard, C.R. (2002) *In the Firing Line. Violence and Power in Child Protection Work.* North Ryde: Wiley.

Storey, J. (1964) 'The Battered Child.' *The Medical Journal of Australia 2*, 789–91.

Strauss, A. and Corbin, J. (1998) *Basics of Qualitative Research. Techniques and Procedures for Developing Grounded Theory.* Thousand Oaks: Sage Publications.

Strenz, T. (1982) 'The Stockholm syndrome: Law enforcement policy and hostage behaviour.' In F.M. Ochberg and D.A. Soskis (eds) *Victims of Terrorism.* Boulder, Colorado: Westview Press, 149–63.

Summit, R.C. (1983) 'The child sexual abuse accommodation syndrome.' *Child Abuse and Neglect 7*, 177–93.

Summit, R.C. (1990) 'The Specific Vulnerability of Children.' In K. R. Oates (ed.) *Understanding and Managing Child Sexual Abuse.* Philadelphia/London: W.B. Saunders/Balliere Tindall, 59–74.

Sykes, J.B. (ed.) (1983) *The Concise Oxford Dictionary of Current English (7th edn).* Oxford: Clarendon Press.

Symonds, M. (1982) 'Victim response to terror: Understanding and treatment.' In F.M. Ochberg and D.A. Soskis (eds) *Victims of Terrorism.* Boulder, Colorado: Westview Press, 95–104.

Terr, L. (1990) *Too Scared to Cry. Psychic Trauma in Childhood.* New York: Harper & Row Publishers.

Thomas, N. and O'Kane, C. (1998) 'The ethics of participatory research with children.' *Children & Society 12*, 336–48.

Thompson, R.A. (1992) 'Developmental changes in research risk and benefit: A changing calculus of concerns.' In B. Stanley and J.E. Sieber (eds) *Social Research on Children and Adolescents.* Newbury Park: Sage Publications, 31–64.

Thurgood, J. (1990) 'Active listening – a social services' perspective.' In A. Bannister, K. Barrett and E. Shearer (eds) *Listening to Children: The Professional Response to Hearing the Abused Child.* Essex, UK: Longman, 51–67.

Tisdall, E.K.M. and Davis, J. (2004) 'Making a difference? Bringing children's and young people's views into policy-making.' *Children & Society 18*, 131–42.

Tomison, A.M. (1996) 'Child maltreatment and family structure.' *Issues in Child Abuse Prevention* (Australian Institute of Family Studies).

Tomison, A.M. (2000) 'Exploring family violence: Links between child maltreatment and domestic violence.' *Issues in Child Abuse Prevention* (Australian Institute of Family Studies), *13*, 1–23.

Tower, C.C. (1989) *Understanding Child Abuse and Neglect.* Massachusetts: Allyn & Bacon.

Tucci, J. (2004) *Towards an Understanding of Emotional and Psychological Abuse: Exploring the Views of Children, Carers and Professionals Involved in the Child Protection System in Victoria.* PhD thesis, Melbourne, Monash University.

Tymchuk, A.J. (1992) 'Assent procedures.' In B. Stanley and J.E. Sieber (eds) *Social Research on Children and Adolescents*. Newbury Park: Sage Publications, 128–42.

United States Advisory Board on Child Abuse and Neglect (1995) *A Nation's Shame: Fatal Child Abuse and Neglect in the United States*. Washington, DC: Department of Health and Human Sciences.

Vondra, J.I. (1990) 'Sociological and Ecological Factors.' In R.T. Ammerman and M. Hersen (eds) *Children at Risk: An Evaluation of Factors Contributing to Child Abuse and Neglect*. New York: Plenum Press, 149–70.

Wales, K. (1996) *Personal Pronouns in Present Day English*. Cambridge: Cambridge University Press.

Wardlaw, G. (1982) *Political Terrorism. Theory, Tactics, and Counter-measures*. Cambridge: Cambridge University Press.

Wardlaw, G. (1989) *Political Terrorism. Theory, Tactics, and Counter-measures* (2nd edn, revised and extended). Cambridge: Cambridge University Press.

Webb, N.B. (1996) *Social Work Practice with Children*. New York: Guilford Press.

Weekes, P. (1994) 'Fatal Inaction', *The Weekend Australian*, 12–13 February.

Weithorn, L.A. and Scherer, D.G. (1994) 'Children's involvement in research participation decisions: psychological considerations.' In M.A. Grodin and L.H. Glantz (eds) *Children as Research Subjects. Science, Ethics and Law*. Oxford: Oxford University Press, 133–79.

Wender, E.H. (1994) 'Assessment of risk to children.' In M.A. Grodin and L.H. Glantz (eds) *Children as Research Subjects. Science, Ethics and Law*. Oxford: Oxford University Press, 181–92.

Wiehe, V.R. (1996) *Working with Child Abuse and Neglect. A Primer*. Thousand Oaks: Sage Publications.

Wilkinson, P. (1987) 'Pathways out of terrorism for democratic societies.' In P. Wilkinson and A.M. Stewart (eds) *Contemporary Research on Terrorism*. Aberdeen: University Press, 453–65.

Wilson, M. (2000) 'Toward a model of terrorist behaviour in hostage-taking incidents.' *Journal of Conflict Resolution 44*, 4, 403–24.

Wilson, M. and Smith, A. (2000) 'Rules and roles in terrorist hostage taking.' In D. Canter and L. Alison, *The Social Psychology of Crime. Groups, Teams and Networks*. Dartmouth: Ashgate, 127–51.

Wise, S. (1995) 'Feminist ethics in practice.' In R. Hugman and D. Smith (eds) *Ethical Issues in Social Work*. London: Routledge, 155–73.

Womack, S. (2003) 'I must tell you more, she cried. But no one listened.' News, Telegraph.co.uk, 29 January.

Wurfel, L.J. and Maxwell, G.M. (1965) 'The "Battered-child Syndrome" in South Australia.' *Australian Paediatric Journal 1*, 127–30.

Zuravin, S.J. (1991) 'Research definitions of child physical abuse and neglect: current problems.' In R.H. Starr Jr and D.A. Wolfe (eds) *The Effects of Child Abuse and Neglect*. New York: Guilford Press, 100–28.

About the Authors

Dr Neerosh Mudaly is a senior counsellor at the Australian Childhood Foundation, where she established the specialized therapeutic service in 1991 for children who have been abused. She has held a number of managerial positions in welfare organizations both in South Africa and Australia. Neerosh has developed particular expertise in working with children who have been abused and with children who engage in problematic sexual behaviours. She has a strong child-centred approach to her practice. Neerosh undertakes education programmes nationally and internationally, and has published in scholarly journals. She is a research fellow at the National Research Centre for the Prevention of Child Abuse at Monash University, where she teaches at undergraduate and postgraduate levels.

Professor Chris Goddard has worked as a social worker in the UK and Australia. He established the first child protection team at the Royal Children's Hospital in Melbourne, Australia. He is the author of a number of books and reports on child abuse and child protection, and has written more than 50 articles on the subject. Chris writes regularly for the media on child protection issues, and is an advocate for children's rights and for the voices of children who have been abused to be heard. His research has led to and contributed to government inquiries and significant media campaigns. He is Head of Social Work and Director of the National Research Centre for the Prevention of Child Abuse in the Faculty of Medicine, Nursing and Health Sciences at Monash University.

Subject Index

Author Index